Praise for **DBT** MADE DOABLE

"What I love most about *DBT Made Doable* is how it makes complex DBT skills feel approachable and immediately applicable. Through clear language, creative implementation strategies, and useful worksheets, it helps clinicians confidently integrate DBT into their work. An invaluable resource for both those new to DBT and experienced practitioners, this book thoughtfully addresses common challenges and offers real-world solutions for bringing DBT skills to life in the counseling room."

—Jasna Koltovska, LMHC, Mental Wellness and Therapy Inc.

"I've collaborated with Lexi for many years and have the privilege of calling her not only a trusted colleague but a dear friend. This book stands out for its ability to make complex DBT concepts feel simple and human—useful for clinicians and accessible to anyone navigating mental health challenges. Lexi has a rare gift for translating dense therapeutic material into something personable, clear, and genuinely useful, making this a book you'll want on your shelf and recommend to others."

—Saul Zalta, LMHC

"Lexi has a remarkable ability to translate complex DBT concepts into practical, accessible tools that clinicians and everyday readers alike can immediately apply. Her engaging teaching style and genuine understanding of how people learn make this book feel approachable without sacrificing depth. Whether you're a clinician looking to integrate DBT more naturally into your practice or someone hoping to build practical DBT skills in your own life, *DBT Made Doable* is an invaluable resource."

—Morgan Nazarzadeh, LMHC

"An empowering and practical resource for therapists. The skills are explained in a clear, accessible way that makes them easy to understand and use right away. This book helps therapists feel more confident bringing these skills into their work with clients in a way that feels natural and authentic rather than clinical. A valuable resource for any therapist looking for practical tools they can use immediately."

—Morgan Stiffler, MSW, LISW-S

DBT
MADE DOABLE

A Clinician's Guide to Teaching Skills That Stick

LEXI MULEE, LMHC

DBT MADE DOABLE

Published by
PESI Publishing, Inc.
3839 White Ave
Eau Claire, WI 54703

Cover and interior design by Emily Dyer
Editing by Jenessa Jackson, PhD

ISBN 9781683739487 (print)
ISBN 9781683739494 (ePUB)
ISBN 9781683739500 (ePDF)

Printed in the United States of America.

PESI Publishing
pesipublishing.com

To all of those who helped me and allowed me to be able to help others. To my mom, dad, and sister, who helped shape the person I am and supported me every step of the way. This book, and the work behind it, exists because of you.

A Note to My Readers

Before we get started, I just want to take a moment to thank all my readers who picked up this book. I know your plate is likely already very full, so adding this to your already busy schedule is something I greatly appreciate, and I feel honored that you are trusting me to walk alongside you as your DBT guide.

I wrote this book for clinicians out there like me, who live and work in the real world. The ones balancing theory with limited time, full caseloads, complex clients, and their own humanity. My hope is that these pages feel less like a dry, crusty textbook and more like something you can actually use—and perhaps even *enjoy* to read. Something that sits next to you, not above you. A gentle reminder that DBT doesn't have to be rigid or intimidating to actually be effective. It can be practical, flexible, and beautifully human!

And in case you ever forget: The work you do deeply matters. On the days it feels invisible, exhausting, or thankless, please know that you make a difference in ways you may never fully see. Thank you for the care, patience, and courage you bring into your clients' lives every day. I hope this book supports you the way DBT has supported me. Let's make it doable!

With so much gratitude,

Lexi

Table of Contents

Introduction

Dialectical behavior therapy (DBT) can feel like a beast. If you've ever opened Marsha Linehan's *DBT Skills Training Manual* and thought, "Where do I even start?" you're not alone! The structure-heavy, step-by-step nature of DBT makes it an incredible framework for treatment, but it can also be intimidating for clinicians who haven't been formally trained in it. And even for those who have, translating DBT skills into real, practical interventions in session can be challenging, to say the least.

That's where this book comes in.

DBT Made Doable is designed for clinicians (hey, that's you!) who want to integrate DBT into their work without feeling like they need to memorize a manual or complete years of specialized training. It is for clinicians at any stage of their career who want to make DBT more natural, realistic, and easy to apply in their sessions. Whether you're a seasoned therapist looking for a no-nonsense way to incorporate DBT skills or a new clinician who wants to learn DBT without feeling overwhelmed, this book was made for you.

DBT: The Great Unknown

Let's be honest: DBT can feel like this big, mysterious thing that no one really knows how to use unless they've had years of training or a PhD in acronyms. I remember my first introduction to DBT as a therapist: sitting in a training, staring at a massive handout packet filled with acronyms and flowcharts and wondering how the hell I was supposed to fit all this into an actual therapy session. It felt like learning a whole new language, and I wasn't sure where to start. And I wasn't alone. So many clinicians I've worked with have told me they love the idea of DBT but felt the same way.

And that's because there's just a lot to it: pages and pages of theory, skills broken down into formulas, a million acronyms, and flowcharts that make you feel like you need a map just to follow them. It's dense. It's a lot to memorize. And even though the skills themselves are amazing, it can feel so hard to figure out how to actually use them in a real therapy session with a real human being sitting in front of you. That's why so many clinicians get overwhelmed by DBT and end up either not using it at all or barely scratching the surface.

On top of that, DBT sometimes comes across as rigid and freakishly structured. In fact, one of the biggest misconceptions about DBT is that it has to look a very specific way. Same language. Same worksheets. Same tone. Same structure. And if you're not doing all that, you're somehow "doing it wrong." YAWN! And more importantly, incorrect.

In reality, that rigidity goes against what DBT is all about: balance, flexibility, and meeting clients where they're at. I view DBT as a framework, not a personality. It was never meant to replace your authentic clinical voice, theoretical orientation, or relational style. It's meant to enhance it. That's exactly why I wrote this book: to cut through all that noise and make DBT feel doable, conversational, and practical!

How to Use This Book: Skill-Per-Page Format Explained

DBT Made Doable uses a skill-per-page format, with each skill broken down in a way that makes sense for both clinicians and clients. For each skill, you'll find a clinician's guide, helping you understand the skill, when to use it, and how to explain it in a way that actually lands with your clients. After that, you'll find a corresponding ready-to-go client worksheet so you can introduce, teach, and apply the skill in real time without spending hours prepping!

This book follows a 30-week DBT curriculum, covering all four core DBT modules: mindfulness, distress tolerance, emotion regulation, and interpersonal effectiveness. These modules (or chapters, if you will) are the foundation of the curriculum, with each offering specific strategies. In addition to these core modules, I have also included two additional skills that are fabulous but don't fit neatly into the modules. The following is an outline of the modules and the skills within each:

Module 1: Mindfulness

- WHAT Skills of Mindfulness
- HOW Skills of Mindfulness
- Mindfulness of the Inner Critic
- Finding Wise Mind
- Practicing a Nonjudgmental Stance
- Cognitive Distortions
- Pocket Mindfulness

Module 2: Distress Tolerance

- Pocket Distress Tolerance (TIPP, STOP, ACCEPTS)
- Five Senses Grounding
- Pros and Cons
- Making Lemonade from Lemons
- Positive/Neutral Coping Thoughts
- Coping Ahead
- Radical Acceptance
- Crisis Survival Strategies When Distress Tolerance Isn't Enough

Module 3: Emotion Regulation

- Identifying Emotions
- PLEASE Skills
- Alternate Rebellion
- Opposite Action
- Checking the Facts
- Problem-Solving
- Behavioral Chain Analysis
- Building Mastery

Module 4: Interpersonal Effectiveness

- The Six Core Interpersonal Effectiveness Skills
- Assertiveness vs. Aggression
- DEAR MAN in Action
- GIVE FAST
- The Emotional Bank Account
- Understanding Boundaries
- Saying No with Confidence
- How to Receive Feedback in a Healthy Way
- Blocks to Interpersonal Effectiveness

Miscellaneous DBT Skills

- Relapse Prevention Plan
- Dialectical Abstinence

You can follow the book's structured flow, moving through each module in order, or pull skills as needed based on your client's goals. Each skill is broken down into simple, digestible steps, using real-world examples, pop culture references (for a bit of fun), and practical applications that make it easy for clients to connect with.

How you teach these skills can and absolutely should vary based on who you are as a clinician and who you're sitting with in the room. Your clinical flavor is what makes these skills land. Not robotic worksheets. Not perfect language. In fact, clients will be able to tell if you try to force language that doesn't naturally fit you. They are very good at sensing whether you're walking the walk or just reciting a textbook. You don't need to sound like a DBT manual. You need to sound like *you*, using DBT concepts intentionally and skillfully.

Remember, this book is not about doing DBT "perfectly." It's about making DBT doable—for you and your clients.

So let's get into it.

A Brief, No-Nonsense Overview of DBT

What is DBT? DBT was originally created in the 1980s by Marsha Linehan for individuals with borderline personality disorder (BPD). It was magnificent in treating specific symptoms such as emotional dysregulation, impulsivity, suicidality, and rocky interpersonal relationships. Although it was intended to be used for folks with BPD, it has proven over the years to be incredibly effective for a range of other struggles, like anxiety, depression, trauma, relationship challenges, and self-destructive behaviors—so in short, it's kind of the GOAT. If you work with clients who struggle with intense emotions, impulsivity, or difficulty navigating relationships, this book will give you the tools and language to help them build skills and create real, actual change in their lives.

DBT works because it's not just theory and it's not just conceptual—it's a genuine toolbox packed with concrete, step-by-step skills that we can practice in real time. These skills help our clients (and ourselves!) regulate their emotions, tolerate distress, communicate effectively, and stay grounded when life gets hard. It's a blend of Eastern mindfulness practices and Western behavioral strategies, giving clients both the mindset and the actionable steps they need to build a life worth living. That's why DBT is so powerful: It meets people exactly where they are while simultaneously showing them how to move forward. What's not to love?!

But how does DBT *actually* work? At its core, DBT combines two things that don't usually go together: acceptance and change. It teaches clients how to accept themselves, their feelings, and their reality as it is right now, while also building the skills to create change in their lives when things aren't working. For example, "This is incredibly painful, and I don't like it (acceptance), and staying exactly the same isn't going to help me build the life I want (*change*)." That dialectic—the both/and thinking—creates a foundation for growth that feels compassionate rather than shame-based.

What Are Dialectics Anyway?

I'm not too proud to admit that I had been practicing DBT, both personally and professionally, for many years before being able to fully and truly wrap my head around what dialectics actually meant. A little embarrassing, but true, and perhaps true for some of you reading this right now!

So what does dialectics mean?

Marsha Linehan defines *dialectics* as "a synthesis or integration of opposites." Which . . . is kind of confusing, right? The simpler way I tend to explain it is "two opposing things can be true at once." But even that can feel a little abstract.

So here's a quick story of when I had a lived experience that helped me fully "get" it. Years ago, a friend of mine had his ninety-something-year-old mother living with him. They were extremely close, and in addition to their emotional bond, he was her full-time caregiver. He did all the things you need to do when you are caring for an elderly loved one. He bathed her, helped her with toileting, made sure she took her medications, kept her comfortable, engaged her intellectually, took her to doctor's appointments—you name it. *All while also* raising two children, supporting his partner, working a full-time job, and managing a household (and two dogs)! He had his hands full, to say the least.

For a few years, it went on like this—month by month, year by year—until his mom passed away in her sleep around age ninety-five. A few days later, I had a moment alone with this friend at the service and asked how he was holding up. He told me with the most earnest face that he was heartbroken and missed his mom so much because in so many ways, she was his best friend. Then his tone dropped a bit and he said, "I'm also feeling a lot of other things that I can't say out loud." I, of course, told him that this was a safe space and that he could tell me what he was feeling if he'd like. And as I'm sure many of you can guess, he shared with me that in addition to grieving, he was feeling a sense of relief. Relief from the heavy, constant burden of caring for an elderly parent. And in that moment—*that* is when I fully got dialectics. If I had been thinking in a black-and-white way, I would have said either he was grieving his mother or feeling relieved—not both. But the truth is, he *was* both. Simultaneously. And equally. That is when I really fully understood what dialectics meant in real life, not just conceptually.

Here are a few more examples of dialectics in real life:

- If you've even been in a toxic relationship, you might have missed that person when you broke up with them, but you also *knew* that they were not the right fit for you.
- A client can actively hate their eating disorder—hate how dangerous it is for them and how it affects their loved ones—while at the same time feeling comfort from these coping skills because they've been using them since they were 13 years old.
- Someone can hate the act of drinking, and even feeling drunk, and at the same time enjoy not having to be present for painful emotions.
- You can love your children more than anything in the world—they can be your sun and your moon!—*and* they are the ones who can drive you the most nuts! Isn't that the truth?

Okay, a few more just to really bring it home:

- You can be very happy for someone and also a bit envious at the same time.
- You can feel sorry about something and not necessarily regret it.
- You can love someone deeply and also know that loving them from a distance is what's safest for you and your mental health. (Relatable much?)

Once you understand that two seemingly opposing things can be true at the same time, it changes how you look at behavior, especially behaviors you're trying to change. A behavior can be harmful *and* have helped us survive. A behavior can keep us stuck *and* once have kept us safe. Holding both truths is essential in DBT.

So let's talk about coping.

Adaptive vs. Maladaptive Coping

Every single one of us has developed strategies to help us survive hard stuff: things like heartbreak, trauma, anxiety, rejection, or that moment you accidentally liked your ex's photo on Instagram. Coping can look like zoning out with Netflix, snapping at someone when we're overwhelmed, avoiding that one email, or drinking more than we meant to. Whatever form it might take, it's important to remember that coping mechanisms didn't come out of nowhere. They were built over time, usually during moments when we didn't have better options.

When someone says, "I know it's not good for me, but it helps," what they're really saying is "This was the best tool I had at the time." And that matters. It matters for us as clinicians to understand so we can lead with compassion, and it matters for our clients to understand so they can begin to step away from shame and self-blame around their "bad habits." Because before we change a behavior, we have to understand its origin, and more often than not, it was about survival.

In DBT, we talk a lot about learning new skills to replace old behaviors, but the truth is, we don't shame the old ones. We honor them. Because they got us through. They worked . . . until they didn't. In some sessions, I even have clients write a love letter to their past maladaptive coping skills, honoring these skills for getting them through a tough time, while also writing a "fuck you" letter to those same coping skills to say, "You're no longer needed." It's very much a "Thank you for your service. You helped me in my past *and* I have better ways now."

And that right there is the key difference between adaptive and maladaptive coping. Adaptive coping helps us stay aligned with our long-term goals and values. It soothes without sabotaging. Maladaptive coping, on the other hand, might feel good in the moment, but it usually adds to our suffering down the line. It's kind of like stuffing unpaid bills in a drawer and pretending they don't exist. It might give us a little relief in the short term, but eventually the electricity gets shut off. Avoidance, numbing, and lashing out might help us dodge discomfort for a moment, but they often create a bigger mess that we have to clean up later.

Now I'll say this: The goal isn't to beat ourselves (or our clients) up for how we've coped. The goal is to get curious: "Did this thing, even if it was harmful, help me survive, or is it helping me live?" Some coping mechanisms were exactly what we needed at one time. They kept us afloat in the middle of the storm. But we're not meant to stay stuck treading water forever. DBT aims to give us the skills not just to stay afloat, but to start swimming with direction, to move toward something better. Something chosen. A life that feels worth living, not just one we're white-knuckling on the daily.

So in short: Maladaptive coping might help in the short term, but it adds to suffering in the long run. Adaptive coping, in contrast, doesn't just help us get through the moment; it helps us build a life that actually feels good to be in.

How to Introduce DBT Skills in a Way That Engages Clients

Most clients don't walk into session and say, "Please teach me a structured evidence-based skill rooted in behavioral theory today!" They usually have one goal, and that goal is to just feel better. Our job as clinicians is to translate the science into something that feels useful, human, and most of all, doable.

When introducing DBT skills, I like to start by making two things really clear:

1. These aren't just "therapy skills." These are life skills. They're practical, they're usable, and truthfully, they actually work.
2. It's a practice. Using one skill one time will not cure you. It takes time, patience, and effort. Just like learning to play the guitar is a skill, so is using DBT. It doesn't happen overnight.

My opinion? Skip the jargon and keep it as real as you can. If you start by calling DBT "a behavioral intervention targeting emotional dysregulation," people's eyes will glaze over, and you'll lose them. Instead, I try to tap into what brought them to therapy in the first place—maybe a relationship that feels stuck, an emotion that feels unbearable, or a pattern they're tired of repeating. Then I link that to the skill. For example, "A lot of people feel like they either explode or shut down when they're upset. This skill gives you a third option."

It's also important to normalize that most of us were never taught this stuff! I'll often say, "No one teaches us how to actually manage emotions or ask for what we need without sounding like a jerk or a doormat. DBT gives us the blueprint for that." This can lighten the self-blame that many clients come into sessions with.

In addition to all this, when I'm introducing DBT skills, I like to tell clients something upfront: Some of these skills are going to sound silly. Like, truly silly. Breathing for five seconds at a time, tipping your head under cold water, saying "I feel . . ." instead of "You always . . ."—it can feel strange or overly simple at first. And I get it, because I felt the same way! But once clients give them a real shot and actually use them, they'll be sold. The skills are surprisingly practical, and more often than not, they work. I'll sometimes say, "I know this sounds stupid, but just give it a go. Let's see if it actually works." Nine times out of ten, the client will tell me later that week that they were annoyed by how well the skill worked, especially compared to how dumb it sounded at first! So I invite clients to be patient, trust the process, and stay open, even to the weird ones. Because even the stupidest sounding skills can end up being the ones that change everything.

And finally, a gentle reminder to keep your language warm, nonclinical, and collaborative. You're not handing down tools from some therapy mountain. You're pulling them out of the toolbox together, testing them out, and figuring out how they can fit into your client's real, messy, beautiful life. DBT is all about being collaborative and working with the client as a true team, so it's vital that the client feels that energy from you, as opposed to a very prescriptive "here, use this skill" type of vibe.

Blending DBT with Other Modalities

DBT skills are fabulous, no doubt about it. They're structured, clear, and often exactly what clients need when things feel chaotic or unmanageable. But let me say this with my full chest: Don't get stuck in a "DBT or bust" mindset. That kind of rigidity actually goes against what DBT stands for at its core, which we know is balance, flexibility, and meeting people where they are at.

You don't need to run a full comprehensive DBT program to use DBT effectively. You can teach one skill when it's needed. You can integrate one concept when it fits. You can pull from DBT when it's clinically indicated and step back when something else is more appropriate. That flexibility is what makes both DBT and your personal clinical practice genuinely effective.

Every clinician has to find their flavor. Their essence. The thing that makes their therapy room feel like a space only they could create. For some of us, that means weaving in bits of ACT to help with cognitive defusion and values-based living. For others, it might be pulling from the Gottman Method when talking about conflict in couples work, or from Internal Family Systems (IFS) therapy when clients are struggling with different internal "parts." It's not cheating on DBT to borrow what works. It's being a thoughtful, flexible, and client-centered therapist, which is what many people need!

Think of it like cooking: DBT is your main dish, but maybe you sprinkle in a little ACT seasoning or plate it with a side of somatic work. The meal becomes your own. As long as you're grounded in why you're choosing what you're choosing, you're on the right track.

As you know, I am a die-hard for DBT skills, *but* I love me some ACT thought defusion. I also have an academic crush on the Gottmans and all the amazing work they've done, and I *love* cognitive behavioral therapy (CBT) interventions. When I bring these techniques into session, I always give a little love to the modality they come from and say something like "This is actually a Gottman technique, but it will be so helpful for making sense of your resentments with your partner. Let's look at it together!" It's good to use different techniques that work for clients' differing needs, not to mention that it models some flexibility in your approach.

So, yes, learn the DBT skills well. Know them. Practice them. But also give yourself permission to mold them into your own special blend. You don't need to become a different therapist to use DBT. You just need to understand the skills well enough to use them with intention, flexibility, and authenticity. And don't forget to bring your amazing self. That's what makes it land, not some annoying acronym.

DBT skills are meant to be malleable, and I hope you'll see that in some of the modules that follow. One skill can be used ten different ways. Take TIPP, for example. It doesn't have to just look like dunking your face in cold water. Instead, it could be holding ice, turning your shower cold for the last few minutes, going outside for a walk in the winter, or holding an ice pack on your vagus nerve. One size does not fit all, my friends! Therapy isn't meant to be robotic; it's meant to be human. And when your clients see you showing up with a full, authentic toolkit that feels like you, they'll feel more empowered to find their own blend too.

MODULE 1

Mindfulness

Mindfulness: The Quick and Dirty

For the moment, take everything you know about mindfulness and put it aside.

For many people, "mindfulness" can be a bit intimidating. It's somewhat vague and also very broad. So let's make it simple. The main goal of mindfulness is two words: SLOW DOWN. Now, you might be thinking, "Okay, but why? Why slow down?" Thought you'd never ask! There are two moments in life when slowing down is key:

1. **In the good moments:** Slowing down in the moments that feel special, exciting, and peaceful allows us to better take it in. Slowing down means we can really savor the moment while creating more stable memories for later recall. Who doesn't want that? Think about the last time you had a really lovely moment. Perhaps it was a moment when your child was being extra cute or silly, or you got the promotion you'd worked so hard for, or you had a quiet morning to enjoy your delicious coffee before the world woke up. These are the good moments you want to savor and *slow down.*
2. **In the uncomfortable moments:** Slowing down helps us focus on using healthy coping skills in the midst of emotional pain instead of giving into impulsive, and possibly damaging, behavior. In these moments, slowing down is like pulling our emergency break. It helps us pause and regain control before things spiral.

Beyond these specific types of moments, slowing down and tapping into mindfulness in general can help us step out of the autopilot mode that we often fall into on a daily basis. Speaking of autopilot, let's try a fun, quick exercise to see how often you operate mindlessly without even realizing it. Check the boxes next to the statements that you identify with. Zero judgment here!

Have you ever:

- ☐ Commuted to school or work and arrived there without remembering the turns or stops you made to get there?
- ☐ Gotten up to get something from another room and then forgotten what you needed when you arrived to said room? And then, of course, you stood there like an idiot.
- ☐ Been unable to remember if you took your routine meds or supplements that day?
- ☐ Been in a conversation and suddenly realized that you have no idea what the other person is talking about because you've been daydreaming?
- ☐ While reading, suddenly realized that you've been thinking about something else and have no idea what you just read for the last four pages?
- ☐ Put something down and then couldn't remember where you just put it?

Mindfulness helps us slow down and get out of autopilot mode. That's really it! It doesn't have to be deeper than that. Mindfulness is flexible, it has range, and it's all about slowing *down*.

It's also important to remember that mindfulness can come in many different forms. It doesn't always have to look like meditation, as if you are *om*-ing in a field of daisies. I think many people are initially turned off to mindfulness because they inaccurately equate it with meditation. Meditation is one form of mindfulness, but don't get it twisted, mindfulness has *range*. It could be as simple as walking in the city and intentionally noticing the architecture of the buildings and the feeling of the sun on your skin, or it could be cooking and really listening to the sound of the veggies sizzling in the pan. Mindfulness is flexible and malleable!

In this module, I'll introduce several tools to help you bring mindfulness into session. Here are some tips to do so without it feeling forced:

- **Start with yourself.** Modeling mindfulness yourself is a great place to start! Grounding before or during the session—like taking a slow breath, noticing the room, or naming what's present for you out loud (e.g., "I'm just taking a second to center before we dive in")—can be powerful for clients to see. They can feel the energy shift when you're genuinely mindful.
- **Sneak it into the flow as best you can.** Instead of announcing, "Let's do a mindfulness exercise," integrate it naturally. For example, you might say, "Before we jump into that, let's take a nice slow breath together" or "Can we pause for a second and notice what emotion just showed up here?"
- **Keep it short and situational.** A twenty-second mindful pause in the middle of a tough story often lands better than a five-minute exercise at the start, especially with clients new to mindfulness. Little pockets of presence go a *long* way!

- **Use language that suits the client.** Some clients will absolutely roll their eyes at "mindfulness" but respond better to "checking in," "slowing down," or "tuning in." Match their language so the practice feels familiar, not foreign.
- **Anchor it in relevance.** Always feel free to explain why you're doing it. Telling clients "This pause helps us get out of autopilot and see what's really going on for you" helps them buy in and connect it to their goals, instead of thinking it's some pointless therapeutic exercise.
- **Notice, don't fix.** Encourage curiosity over correction. If a client says, "I can't stop thinking," respond with "Perfect, that's noticing! That's mindfulness."
- **Use the environment around you.** Have clients notice sounds from the hallway, the feel of the chair, or their breath. Everyday anchors keep mindfulness real and unpretentious, and most importantly—accessible.
- **Normalize awkwardness!** When clients say, "This feels weird," agree with them! "Yeah, slowing down can feel weird at first, but that's the point. We spend most of our lives on fast-forward, so let's embrace the weird!"
- **End with reflection.** You can ask, "What did you notice?" rather than "Did it work?" to keep curiosity alive instead of judgment.
- **Keep your tone light.** Humor and warmth keep mindfulness human. It doesn't need candles or silence—just gentle presence.

WHAT Skills of Mindfulness

Learning how to pay attention on purpose

Observe | Describe | Participate

In DBT, mindfulness is broken down into WHAT skills and HOW skills. The WHAT skills tell us what to actually *do* when we're being mindful. Think of these as the behaviors of mindfulness, and they always happen one at a time. Just one. Not two. Not all three. One at a time, because the goal is presence, not performance.

Let's break them down.

Observe

This is about noticing, without having to do anything about what we notice. No labeling, judging, or fixing. It's just paying attention to what's happening both around us and inside us. This can feel quite uncomfortable for clients at first, especially those with heightened nervous systems or posttraumatic stress disorder, particularly if they're used to reacting right away or avoiding internal experiences. But observing is the first step toward gaining awareness.

When you're teaching this skill, encourage clients to gently notice the physical sensations in their body, the sounds around them, their breath, their emotions, or their thoughts, without needing to analyze or respond. You might say, "Let's practice being a gentle observer here. Imagine your thoughts are like clouds and you're just lying in the grass, watching them float by."

Pro tip: Start with external observations (sounds, sights, sensations) before moving inward. It's less threatening for some clients.

Describe

Once your client has observed something, the next skill is to put words to it. Describing means naming what we just observed without judgment. The goal isn't to label everything as good or bad—it's to build clarity and language around our internal experiences. This helps clients slow their roll a bit and create space between noticing and reacting. Here is some sample language you can model:

- "I noticed a tightness in my chest and had the thought 'I can't handle this.'"
- "I noticed my face getting hot and the thought 'I might have said the wrong thing.'"

This step is where clients start to feel some mastery over their emotional experiences, because naming gives form to the formless. It also begins to separate them from the storm they're in.

Common sticking point: Clients will often describe their experiences using judgmental language (e.g., "I felt dumb," "I was being annoying"). When this happens, gently redirect them to stick to the facts and use neutral language:

CLINICIAN: "What did you notice that led you to think that?"

CLIENT: "I noticed my friend's facial expression changed, and I had the thought that I was 'being annoying.'"

Participate

Participate is about diving in—*fully*. It's the opposite of dissociating, overthinking, or half-showing-up. When we participate, we let ourselves become one with the moment instead of holding back. It can be dancing without worrying about how we look, laughing at a joke without editing our reaction, or working on a creative project without mentally checking out to scroll through our phone. In short, it's about being fully present with life as it's happening.

Clients who are anxious or perfectionistic, or those who are trauma survivors, may struggle with this WHAT skill. It can feel scary to drop the guardrails, and understandably so. But when done in bite-sized, safe ways, participating helps build trust within the self and the present moment.

You can sell this skill as "accessing your flow state." Encourage clients to identify activities where they already do this—maybe playing an instrument, painting, or engaging with pets or kids. You can build from there!

Using the WHAT Skills in Session

These skills can be practiced right in the therapy room. You might invite your client to pause, observe three things in the room, describe one internal feeling without judgment, and then fully participate in a short grounding or emotion-focused exercise. I always tell clients it's great to start incorporating these skills in non-emotionally charged situations, build up their skills, and use them in more challenging situations as they improve!

Over time, clients can learn that mindfulness isn't just about sitting in silence on a meditation cushion. It's about strengthening their attention muscle so they can stay present without being overwhelmed by what they notice. And that presence is what allows space for change—more to come there!

Client Worksheet

WHAT Skills of Mindfulness

Learning how to pay attention on purpose

Observe | Describe | Participate

Mindfulness means paying attention to the present moment on purpose, without judgment. The WHAT skills tell you "what to do" when you're practicing mindfulness. Let's walk through each one together.

Observe

Just notice. That's it. You don't have to do anything else right now. Just tune into your experience like you're watching a movie or listening to a song: no reacting, no judging, no fixing. Take a moment right now and simply observe what's going on. Try not to change or judge anything. Just notice.

Describe

Now that you've observed, put words to what you just noticed. Describe things without adding opinions or judgments. Try to stick to neutral language and avoid words like "bad," "wrong," or "should." Just the facts here. Use this sentence starter to help guide you: "I noticed . . ."

What did you see around you?

____

____

What did you hear?

____

____

What did you feel in your body?

____

____

What emotions or thoughts showed up?

____

____

Participate

This is about jumping in fully. Instead of watching from the sidelines, imagine diving headfirst into the experience you are having right now! No holding back. No multitasking. Just be in it.

What's one activity you can fully participate in today (no distractions, no phones)?

What would it look like to be fully present in that activity?

What gets in the way of fully participating? How can you gently notice and let go of that?

Final Reflection

How did it feel to observe, describe, and participate? Which skill felt the most natural to you? Which one felt more challenging?

HOW Skills of Mindfulness

Learning how to pay attention on purpose

Nonjudgmentally | One-Mindfully | Effectively

Now that your clients know what to do to be mindful (observe, describe, participate), the HOW skills teach them *how* to do it! Think of it like this: If the WHAT skills are the ingredients, the HOW skills are the recipe and instructions on how to cook. They give us the attitude, the posture, and the spirit from which mindfulness is practiced.

These three skills—nonjudgmentally, one-mindfully, and effectively—can be especially helpful for clients who tend to get discouraged or say, "I'm doing this wrong." Spoiler alert: There is no wrong way to be mindful, as long as you're doing it with these HOW skills in mind!

Nonjudgmentally

Let's get one thing straight from the jump: Nonjudgmentally doesn't mean never having a judgmental thought (we're human, not robots). It more realistically means noticing those judgments when they show up and practicing letting them pass without clinging, reacting, or spiraling. The idea is to observe the judgment as a judgment, not as a truth.

Since clients often confuse judgments with descriptions, it's important to help them tease these apart:

JUDGMENT: "I'm being lazy."

DESCRIPTION: "I've been lying on the couch for three hours."

JUDGMENT: "She's being rude."

DESCRIPTION: "She ended the call without saying goodbye."

The more clients practice observing judgments like passing clouds—"Oh hey, there's a judgment" and "Oh, there it is again!"—the less power those thoughts hold.

Session tip: If a client judges their emotional response (e.g., "I shouldn't feel this way"), gently pause and invite them to notice that thought as just a judgment—not a fact—and then return back to describing.

One-Mindfully

This is the practice of doing one thing at a time with our full attention. In a culture that *glorifies* multitasking, this skill feels almost radical in a weird way. But the truth is, multitasking fragments our attention and leaves us feeling frazzled, disconnected, unsatisfied, and possibly frustrated.

One-mindfully is about putting all our mental energy into the *one* task at hand, whether it's eating, walking, talking, or brushing our teeth. Even if what we're doing feels boring or uncomfortable, this skill is about staying with it and not splitting our awareness. I like to joke with my clients and tell them that instead of doing ten things half-assed, they should pick one of those things and do it with their full ass!

Bonus reframe: This skill also helps clients stay grounded in emotionally charged situations. By one-mindfully reminding themselves, "Right now, I'm just listening" or "Right now, I'm just breathing," they can reduce reactivity and avoid spinning out.

Effectively

This skill is such a gem because it gently calls out perfectionism, stubbornness, and emotional reasoning—in the best way. Effectively means doing what works for you, not what you wish would work, or what you think should work, or what your anxiety is screaming at you to do.

Think of it like this: Who reading this enjoys meditation? I'm sure some of you will say, "Oh, I do!" and an equal amount will say, "Not me!" I would argue that many people who don't like meditation were told at some point in their lives "You have to get into this! It's transformative and *so* helpful!" But for many people, meditation isn't that. It's anxiety-provoking, boring, or just simply not effective.

Doing what is effective means letting go of what we "think" should work or what everyone else says is the "right" thing do. It means no longer white-knuckling our way through it and, instead, choosing something that actually does work for us. It might sound stupid, but doing what's effective is very much "Stop trying to make fetch happen!" from *Mean Girls*. Do not force something on you that doesn't work. It's a waste of time and energy. Instead, find the skills that do work and master them. Don't let your pride or emotions hijack your goals. Stay flexible, stay goal-oriented, and do what moves you—operative word being *you*—forward.

For clients, this might mean skipping meditation and going for a walk because that works better for them. It might mean walking away from an argument even though they want to "win." It might mean using *opposite action* (a skill from the emotion regulation module) even when it feels unnatural, because it gets them closer to their values.

Session tip: Come back to this question often: "What's the most effective move right now for your goal? Not the most dramatic, not the most righteous, and not the one you 'think' you should be using. Just the most effective."

HOW Skills of Mindfulness

Learning how to pay attention on purpose

Nonjudgmentally | One-Mindfully | Effectively

The HOW skills teach you how to practice mindfulness in a way that actually helps you feel better, stay grounded, and build awareness without spinning out. These three skills are the mindset and attitude you bring into mindfulness. Let's explore each one.

Nonjudgmentally

We all have judgments. It's human! This skill is about noticing those judgments and letting them go instead of grabbing on and spiraling. Think about a moment today where a judgmental thought came up. Try to slow it down and reflect.

What was the situation?

____

____

What judgmental thought popped up?

____

____

Now try rewriting that judgment as a nonjudgmental observation: "Instead of saying ______________ ______________________, I could say, ______________________________________."

How did it feel to shift that language?

____

____

One-Mindfully

This skill is all about doing *one* thing at a time, with your full attention, instead of trying to split your focus on multitasking. It helps calm the chaos, cut through the overwhelm, and create some presence. Let's practice.

What's one thing you did today while multitasking?

____

____

What would it have looked like to do that one-mindfully?

____

____

Choose one small activity you can try doing one-mindfully today (e.g., brushing your teeth, walking the dog, eating a snack, watching your show). After doing it, how did it feel to stay with that experience fully?

____

____

Effectively

Effectively means doing what works, not what you wish would work, or what "should" work, or what you feel like doing in the moment. It's all about acting in a way that moves you toward your goals!

What's a recent situation where you used a skill that you thought should work, but it actually didn't help?

____

____

What would have been a more effective choice in that moment?

____

____

What are some strategies you think or wish would work for you, but in all reality, don't?

____

____

What's one strategy you can use when you catch yourself getting stuck in "this should work" mode that might actually work better?

____

____

Complete this sentence: "Even though I feel like I should __________________________,

the most effective thing I can do right now is __________________________."

Final Reflection

Which HOW skill felt the most natural to you? Which one felt more challenging? How might practicing these skills help you handle challenges a bit differently moving forward?

Mindfulness of the Inner Critic

How to notice the inner critic without believing everything it says

A frustrating truth: Every one of us has an inner critic. It's that voice in our head that's convinced it's helping by pushing us to do better, be better, and look better, but instead, it just makes us feel like garbage. The inner critic is sneaky. It doesn't shout. It whispers—secretly shaping our moods, our view of ourselves and others, and the way we navigate the world. Often, we don't even realize it's operating in the background until we name it.

So why include this work in the mindfulness module?

Because mindfulness is about being aware—without judgment. Before we can challenge something, we first have to notice it's happening. This skill helps clients bring a gentle, curious awareness to the harsh inner monologue running the show and, little by little, start talking back to it.

Keep in mind that we're not trying to kill the inner critic. We're trying to understand where it came from, separate from it a bit, and respond to it with compassion and clarity instead of just absorbing it like truth.

To introduce this concept to clients, start by explaining what the inner critic is and why we want to draw some awareness to it:

> *"The inner critic is that internal voice that tells us we're not enough—not smart enough, not attractive enough, not productive enough, not likable enough. It speaks in absolutes. The inner critic is insidious—affecting how we think, feel, and behave—but we often don't even realize it's operating in the background until we name it. Even though it's wildly unhelpful, the inner critic tends to operate under the guise of protection by reminding us of our greatest fears: our potential for hurt, our disappointments from the past, and our fears about the future. While it may have formed as a protective mechanism—trying to keep us from getting hurt or rejected by pushing us to be better, smaller, or safer—over time, this voice often becomes harsh, rigid, and damaging."*

Then walk the client through the steps of noticing and challenge their inner critic.

Step 1: Identify What the Inner Critic Is Saying

Start by getting curious: What's the narrative? What message is the inner critic sending? Is it about the client's body, competence, or worth as a partner, parent, or human? You can invite clients to complete the sentence: "My inner critic often tells me _____." This step is just about naming. The client doesn't have to do anything about it yet. You're just shining a flashlight on the cobwebs.

Step 2: Switch to "You," Not "I"

This one feels weird at first, but it works. When a client says, "I'm a failure," ask them to try flipping it to "You're a failure." Why? Because hearing it from that angle can externalize the voice and reveal how cruel it actually sounds. Often, when clients say these things out loud—as if someone else were saying it to them—they instinctively want to protest. That's a good sign that reflects Wise Mind (more on that later) stepping in!

Step 3: Identify Where It's Coming From

Here's where you help clients trace the voice back to its roots. Is that voice echoing something a parent used to say? A teacher? A mean kid in middle school? Or maybe it was modeled to them, like hearing a parent call themselves "disgusting" and absorbing that language over time. Try asking, "Where do you think your inner critic got its material?" This is less about blame and more about insight. When clients know where this voice came from, they can see it for what it is: a learned message, not a universal truth.

Step 4: Personify the Inner Critic

This is where you can get a bit playful. Ask your client, "If your inner critic had a name, what would it be? What would it wear? What would it sound like? What would it look like?" One of my clients called hers "Regina George," the queen bee from *Mean Girls*. Another called his "Sergeant Hartman," the crazy intense drill sergeant from *Full Metal Jacket* who would yell and invalidate his every emotion, behavior, and experience. I know clients might roll their eyes at this, but in all honesty, giving it a character gives them distance. It helps them talk *to* it, rather than *as* it. It also adds a little humor, which lightens the emotional load. Who doesn't want that?

Step 5: Answer Back Using "I"

Now that you know what the critic is saying and who it's pretending to be, it's time to talk back to it. And here's the thing: You're not doing a toxic positivity exercise with fairy tale affirmations that don't stick. You're aiming for something that's grounded and kind. Something that actually resonates. That means if the client's critic says, "You look disgusting in that outfit," the response isn't "I look amazing and love every part of myself." (Because if that doesn't feel true, it won't help.) Instead, it might be "I don't love how I look today, but I'm learning to speak to myself more gently" or "This outfit doesn't feel great, and that's okay. I'm still worthy of respect and care." You want this response to sound like a wise, loving friend stepping in, not a motivational speaker that the client rolls their eyes at. Invite your client to write their own: "How will you answer back to your inner critic speaking from the point of view 'I'?"

After walking through these steps, some clients may still struggle to believe kinder statements about themselves. They may say, "I can tell myself 'I'm a good person' all I want, but what if I just don't believe it?" In this case, you can share information about neuroplasticity to normalize why it feels hard and illustrate that change *is* possible:

> *"That's okay! It's understandable that your heart won't be in it if you have been telling yourself negative things your whole life and all of a sudden try to flip the script. But this is where neuroplasticity comes into play! Your brain is not a fixed machine; it's constantly rewiring itself based on what you repeatedly think, feel, and do. That's called neuroplasticity. When you keep*

telling yourself the same harsh, critical thoughts over and over—like 'I'm not good enough' or 'I always mess things up'—your brain strengthens those neural pathways. They become automatic and fast, and they feel true even if they're not facts.

Now, when you start interrupting those thoughts, even if it feels weird or forced at first (which it will!), you're literally starting to build new neural pathways. It's like going from a deeply rutted trail in the woods to slowly stomping out a new path. At first, it's clunky. It doesn't feel natural. But with repetition, the new thoughts start to become more accessible and believable. You're not erasing the old path right away, but you're choosing not to keep deepening it.

And remember, this isn't about toxic positivity or pretending everything's okay. It's about saying, 'Hey, maybe there's another way to see this. Maybe I don't have to bully myself every time I mess up.' You don't have to 100 percent believe a reframe for it to be effective. You just have to be willing to practice it. That's the difference between being stuck in shame and building a new response. So, no, it's not 'fluff.' It's reps. It's like going to the gym for your brain. And you don't have to do it perfectly—you just have to be willing to show up and practice!"

If clients are still struggling to find the words to be kind to themselves, invite them to pretend that they are talking to a loved one. If their best friend called and said they hated being sensitive, or were struggling with their body image, chances are the client would respond with empathy and support—and also help the friend see a less harsh and more loving perspective. Encourage the client to try this on themselves the next time the inner critic rears its ugly head.

Mindfulness of the Inner Critic

How to notice the inner critic without believing everything it says

Before we dive in, let's talk about that voice in your head.

You know the one: The running commentary. The unsolicited opinions. The harsh little narrator who pops up the second you make a mistake or feel unsure of yourself.

That's your inner critic.

Now, here's something important to remember: The inner critic is not the enemy. It usually develops for a reason. At some point in your life, being hard on yourself may have felt protective, or maybe the inner critic thought it was keeping you motivated. Maybe it learned those messages from someone else. Maybe it believed that if it criticized you first, no one else could hurt you.

The problem is that over time, that voice can get louder, more convincing. And mean.

This worksheet is not about getting rid of your inner critic. It's about learning to notice it without automatically believing everything it says. We're building space between you and the thought. Because a thought is just that—a thought, not a fact. And just because your brain says something in a confident tone does not make it true.

Think of this as strength training for your mind. We're doing reps. The goal is not perfection. The goal is practice.

Let's meet your inner critic. And then let's learn how to talk back.

Step 1: What Is Your Inner Critic Saying?

What are some things your inner critic tends to say to you? (Examples: "I always mess things up," "I'm not emotionally resilient," "People think I'm stupid")

____

____

____

Step 2: Flip It—Use "You" Instead of "I"

Take one of the statements from step 1 and rewrite it using "you" instead of "I." (Example: "You always mess things up")

____

____

____

Step 3: Where Did Your Inner Critic Learn These Messages?

Where do you think these kinds of thoughts originally came from? A person? An experience? Something you heard growing up?

____

____

____

Step 4: If Your Inner Critic Was a Person or Character, Who Would It Be?

Give your inner critic a name and describe it. What does it sound like? Look like? (Examples: "Regina George from *Mean Girls*," "My seventh-grade gym teacher")

Name: ______________________________

Description: ______________________________

Step 5: What Would You Say Back to Your Inner Critic?

Answer back to one of your inner critic's statements using a realistic and compassionate statement framed from a first-person point of view. (Example: "I don't always get it right, but I'm doing my best")

____

____

____

Hold on to this worksheet for the next time that inner critic rears its ugly head, and remember to reframe as best you can in the moment, even if it doesn't fully feel believable. Remember, it's about doing reps!

Finding Wise Mind

A practical guide to balancing emotion and logic

Wise Mind is a phrase you've probably heard a million times, but what does it *actually* mean? Wise Mind is one of the three states of mind in DBT: Emotional Mind, Rational Mind, and Wise Mind. It's the ability to pause, reflect, and access a more balanced perspective in emotionally charged or confusing situations. It's also super useful when we're trying to make big decisions.

Wise Mind is one of the most foundational DBT skills. It helps clients step back and evaluate their thoughts, feelings, and decisions from a place that honors *both* emotion and logic. It's the opposite of a knee-jerk emotional reaction or cold detachment. Wise Mind is that centered place that feels right and makes sense. In many ways, it's likened to our "gut." You can introduce it like this to clients:

> *"In DBT, we believe that everyone has three states of mind. We all have an Emotional Mind that's driven by urges and feelings. We all also have a Rational Mind that's driven by facts and logic. And then we have the in-between—the both/and—and that's our Wise Mind. Consider Wise Mind to be the overlap of both Emotional Mind and Rational Mind. It's our intuition, our inner quiet knowing, the part of us that knows what's right, even if it's hard."*

Explaining Emotional Mind

> *"Emotional Mind is that part of us that's reactive and urgent. This portion of our mind is mood dependent, hot-tempered, and obviously, emotion focused. When we are in Emotional Mind, we are typically ruled by our urges, moods, and feelings. You might use your Emotional Mind for arguing with a loved one, falling in love, or using mood-altering substances. All things that take emotion into account, but not so much logic, right?"*

Explaining Rational Mind

> *"On the other side of things, we have our Rational Mind. Some people call this Logic Mind or Reasonable Mind, but it's all the same gist. This side of our mind is rational, calm, task focused, and calculated. When we are in this type of headspace, we are ruled by facts, logic, and pragmatics. You might use your Rational Mind for creating a monthly budget, following directions to a new part of town, or organizing your schedule for the week. All things you don't really need to consider emotions for, right?"*

Explaining Wise Mind

> *"Wise Mind is the sweet spot in the middle. It's essentially a mental middle ground where we are able to see the value of both our emotions and logic in any given experience and make decisions in a clear and healthy way. This is where we can pause, feel our feelings, think through*

our options, and respond in a way that aligns with our values. This captures the balanced essence that we are always striving toward in DBT!"

If clients are visual learners, you can draw a simple Venn diagram on a whiteboard with two circles labeled Emotional Mind and Rational Mind, with Wise Mind in the middle. If you want to have a little fun with it, you can use pop culture anchors! For example, you can say, "Think of Rational Mind like Spock from *Star Trek*—calculated and cool. Emotional Mind is more like Maddy from *Euphoria*—passionate, impulsive, and deep in her feels. Wise Mind is your inner Yoda. Calm. Centered. All-knowing."

Use a Real-Life Scenario in Session

Once the framework is clear, bring it to life using a real-life scenario the client is struggling with. Invite them to talk through a tough decision or situation they're facing where it's clear they are either stuck in Emotional Mind or Rational Mind. You can break it down like this:

- *"Okay, so what is your Emotional Mind saying right now?" Follow that up with: "What's its 'call to action'? In other words, what is it urging you to do or act on?"*
- *"Now, let's flip it. Even if it feels harder to connect to, what would your Rational Mind say if it could weigh in on the topic?" Again ask, "What's the call to action here?"*
- *"Now, let's slow it down with a steady breath. Let's be present in this moment." Remind them: "Wise Mind is a place where both emotions and logic come together. It's not about ignoring your feelings or cutting off your thoughts. It's about integrating both so you can make a decision that feels right in your gut and is also reasonable. What does your Wise Mind say here?"*

If they're stuck in one mind or the other, suggest they talk it out with someone who tends to live in the opposite mind, or this could be your opportunity to role-play that moment in session! This can shake up their perspective and make space for balance. You can also offer these reflection questions to support clients in understanding if they are achieving Wise Mind:

- *"Do you feel calm, grounded, and connected to your inner values?"*
- *"Are you balancing your emotions with facts and logic right now?"*
- *"Does this decision or thought align with what truly matters to you?"*
- *"Are you able to accept this moment as it is, without fighting or avoiding it?"*
- *"Do you feel confident that this decision is something you'll be proud of later?"*
- *"Can you sense your inner wisdom, even if the decision is hard or uncomfortable?"*

If a client is struggling to tell the difference between their gut and their anxiety, here is what I would consider saying:

> *"Wise Mind doesn't usually scream. Anxiety does. When it's anxiety talking, there's often this panicky urgency, like you have to solve the problem right now or something terrible will happen. It feels loud, overwhelming, and rushed. Wise Mind, on the other hand, is quieter. It's more of a calm knowing that sits patiently in the background. It doesn't push or panic. It gently offers clarity, even if the answer it gives is hard. It usually feels grounded and steady, not frantic or desperate. If the voice in your head is sounding like a fire alarm, it's probably not Wise Mind. If it's quiet but confident, like something you just know deep down, it's likely Wise Mind."*

You can also offer a body-based check-in:

> *"Where do you feel this message in your body? Anxiety often shows up in the chest, shoulders, or stomach. It feels tight, heavy, clenched. Wise Mind tends to feel steadier and more centered, often a bit lower in the body or around the heart space. It feels like exhaling after holding your breath."*

Don't get it twisted. Wise Mind isn't always a peaceful feeling. Sometimes it's uncomfortable. In fact, *many* times it's uncomfortable. But it tends to feel *right*, even if clients aren't fully ready to admit or acknowledge it. At the end of the day, Wise Mind choices align with our values, not just our comfort. They reflect the kind of person we want to be, not just what would bring the quickest relief in the moment. Wise Mind asks, "What matters to me long term?" instead of "What will make this feeling go away right now?"

Client Worksheet

Finding Wise Mind

A practical guide to balancing emotion and logic

When we're overwhelmed, we tend to default to extremes. Emotional Mind says, "Do something right now. Make it stop," while Rational Mind says, "Feelings are inconvenient. Let's just solve this problem strategically."

Wise Mind is that place inside of us where emotion and logic meet. It honors what we're feeling while simultaneously considering the facts at hand. Then it responds from a place that is grounded, intentional, and aligned with who we actually want to be.

This worksheet is designed to slow things down and help you look at a situation you're facing from a Wise Mind perspective. Instead of reacting on autopilot, you're going to walk through each state of mind step by step. The goal is to create enough space to choose your response wisely. Take your time with it. Breathe as you go.

What's the Situation?

Take a moment to briefly describe the situation you're facing right now. What's happening? Try to be as detailed as you can.

____

____

What Is Your Emotional Mind Saying?

Let's tap into your Emotional Mind. What thoughts and feelings are coming up? What is your Emotional Mind saying to you?

____

____

Call to Action: What Is Emotional Mind Urging You to Do?

What action does your Emotional Mind want you to take right now?

____

____

What Is Your Rational Mind Saying?

Now, let's try to switch gears. What facts are present? What is your logical, task-focused mind saying?

____

____

Call to Action: What Is Rational Mind Urging You to Do?

What would your Rational Mind have you do next?

What Is Your Wise Mind Saying?

Now, center and ground yourself for a moment. Pause. Breathe. Imagine stepping into a place that honors both your emotions and your logic. What does your Wise Mind say here?

How Does That Wise Mind Response Feel in Your Body?

As you consider this response, scan your body and notice what you feel internally. Do you feel more grounded? Anxious? Calm? Confident?

Does This Decision Align with Your Values?

Check in with what matters to you. Does this choice align with your values and the goals you are working toward?

Would You Be Proud of This Decision Later?

Think ahead. When you imagine looking back at this decision, does it feel like something future-you would feel good about?

"Emotions are always valid. Logic is useful. But your deepest truth lives where they meet."

—Lexi Mulee (because why not!)

Practicing a Nonjudgmental Stance

Noticing without labeling things as good or bad

Judgments keep us stuck. They narrow our perspective, fuel emotional reactivity, and often make us feel worse—about ourselves, about others, about life. When we're judging, we're not in the moment. We're usually in our heads, spiraling.

But let's get one thing out of the way: We all judge. All. The. Time. It's not a character flaw—it's just how our brains work. Our minds are wired to scan, label, and categorize information as quickly as possible to keep us safe and efficient. In fact, Carl Jung once said, "Thinking is difficult, that's why most people judge." And honestly, he's kind of right if you think about it. Judging is easy: Our brains are hardwired to make quick, automatic judgments about things so we can move through the world without spending too much time or energy overthinking every little thing. Understanding, on the other hand, is harder because it requires deep thinking, patience, compassion, and an open mind. We are built for efficiency, babe!

So when I talk about adopting a nonjudgmental stance, I'm not saying that clients should never have another judgmental thought again—because that's not realistic or sustainable! Instead, this skill invites them to notice their judgments as they arise (about themselves, others, or the world) and observe them with curiosity rather than criticism. From there, they can gently pivot away from the judgment and turn back toward awareness, compassion, and the facts of the current moment. It's kind of like saying, "Hi, judgment, I see you, I hear you, *and* now I'm going to focus back on the present moment."

In addition, clients don't have to approve of everything or turn into passive doormats to practice a nonjudgmental stance. It's more like learning to observe reality without piling on the emotional weight of "shoulds," labels, and assumptions. That frees them up to respond with more clarity, compassion, and intention—and then get back to the good stuff: the present moment! Here are the steps to introduce and practice this skill.

Step 1: Normalize That Judgments Are Completely Human

Start by reminding your clients that we all make judgments, and there's no shame in that! We all have a little Larry David in us somewhere.

Step 2: Identify Judgment Patterns

Next, encourage your clients to look for themes within their judgments. Do they judge themselves more, or others? When judgments pop up, what are common themes? Are they about other people's appearances, work ethic, emotional expressiveness, or relationship status? Or are they about themselves: how they look, what they say, how they feel? Naming these patterns helps bring them into awareness, and awareness is the first step toward change.

Step 3: Ask, "Is This Judgment Helping or Hurting?"

This simple question invites clients to reflect on whether their judgment is serving a helpful purpose—like setting a boundary or guiding a decision—or if it's just keeping them stuck. For example, judging someone's outfit or appearance probably won't help them build meaningful connections. But noticing that a situation feels unsafe and trusting that gut instinct? That's protective—and absolutely allowed.

To help clients figure out the difference, invite them to notice the function of the judgment: "Is this judgment guiding you toward a value, like safety, respect, or well-being? Or is it pulling you away from the present moment and making you feel worse?"

If the judgment leads to constructive action, like asserting a boundary, protecting themselves, or making an informed choice, it may be helpful. If it leads to spiraling, shame, avoidance, disconnection, or reinforcement of an old critical narrative, it's likely a harmful judgment.

Step 4: Shift the Language

Words matter! Here, you want to guide clients to rephrase their judgmental thought into a statement of preference or fact. Instead of "My coworkers are the worst," try, "I wish I felt more connected to the people I work with." Instead of "My boss hates me," try, "He gave me direct feedback about my presentation." Language like this softens the emotional charge and keeps us grounded in reality.

Step 5: Don't Judge the Judgment

Here's the paradox: Clients will inevitably start judging themselves for being judgmental. And you know what? That's okay and to be expected! Help them notice that too, and let it pass. Remind them that even noticing a judgment is a small win. It means they're paying attention, which is exactly what mindfulness is all about, so kudos on the noticing!

Step 6: Practice Having a "Beginner's Mind"

Beginner's mind is a concept in DBT that helps clients approach situations as if they're experiencing them for the *very* first time. It's a powerful antidote to prejudgment. For example, if a client finds themselves getting "pre-annoyed" before a family dinner because of past experiences, a beginner's mind invites them to say, "This is a new dinner, on a new day, with new energy. Let's see what happens if I approach it with a blank slate. People might surprise me (or I might even surprise myself!)."

Optional homework: Suggest that clients complete a Weekly Judgment Log. Each time a judgment pops up, have them jot it down, along with the context and any accompanying physical or emotional reactions. This builds insight and naturally creates more space between thought and reaction.

Client Worksheet

Practicing a Nonjudgmental Stance

Noticing without labeling things as good or bad

We all judge . . . ourselves, other people, situations, even our own feelings. This skill isn't about never having another judgmental thought again (that's not possible, so no pressure!). Instead, it's about noticing those judgments when they show up, pausing, and choosing to come back to the moment with curiosity instead of criticism.

Step 1: What Do You Tend to Judge?

Let's start by building awareness. Think about what your judgments are usually about. Fill in what feels true for you.

I tend to judge myself about . . .

____

I tend to judge other people about . . .

____

I tend to judge the world/situations about . . .

____

Step 2: Pick One Recent Judgment You've Had

Think of one judgment you've had recently that really stuck with you. What was the judgment?

____

____

Who or what was it about?

____

____

How did it affect you (emotionally, physically, behaviorally)?

____

____

Step 3: Is This Judgment Helping or Hurting?

Let's get curious, not critical. Ask yourself:

- ☐ Did this judgment help you take action that aligned with your values?
- ☐ Or did it just make you feel worse, more stuck, or disconnected?

Explain your answer:

____

____

What value (if any) were you trying to protect or express with this judgment? (Examples: safety, honesty, connection, respect)

____

____

Step 4: Try Reframing It

Let's try reframing that judgment into either:

- A statement of preference (e.g., "I wish . . .," "I'd rather . . .," "It'd be nice if . . . ")
- A statement of fact (e.g., "This happened in this way at this time . . . ")

Your original judgment:

____

____

Your reframe:

____

____

How does it feel to say it that way instead?

____

____

Step 5: Be Gentle with Yourself

Did you notice that you judged yourself for having judgment? If so, that's okay too! Write any self-criticism you noticed.

____

____

What is a supportive or compassionate statement you could say to yourself instead? (Examples: "This is a habit I'm working on," "I'm human," "Noticing is a win")

____

____

Step 6: Practice a Beginner's Mind

Choose one upcoming situation in which you tend to prejudge. Let's write a new way to approach it:

Old thought: "I already know how this will go because ______________________________

____."

New thought with a beginner's mind: "I'm going to treat this as a brand-new experience and stay open to ____

____."

Optional Practice: Weekly Judgment Log

This week, track any judgmental thoughts you notice and how they impacted your mood, body, or behavior. Don't try to change them—just notice.

Day	Judgment	What Triggered It	How It Made You Feel

Cognitive Distortions

How to start recognizing unhelpful thinking patterns

Cognitive distortions . . . what are they exactly? The long and the short of it is that they are distorted thinking patterns that pull us out of the present moment and into inaccurate or self-critical stories.

Cognitive distortions are *technically* a CBT skill, but they fit perfectly in the DBT mindfulness module because distorted thoughts yank us out of the moment. Mindfulness is all about noticing reality as it is, without judgment. When clients fall into catastrophizing, black-and-white thinking, or overgeneralizing, they aren't really present with what's actually happening—they're tangled up in their mind's stories and twisted narratives. It's as if they're wearing glasses with the wrong prescription. Everything looks a bit blurrier and feels more threatening than it really is. Clients often don't realize they're even engaging in these distortions because the thoughts can feel so real in the moment! But these patterns tend to drag them (and us!) out of the here and now, fuel intense emotions, and create suffering on top of suffering.

When we can teach clients to identify these distortions, it helps them mindfully notice thoughts as just thoughts—not facts. It isn't about erasing or fighting thoughts. It's about inviting clients to notice when a thought is distorted, label it as such, and consider a gentler or more balanced reframe. This is a direct pathway back to Wise Mind instead of Emotional Mind, and who doesn't want that?

To teach this skill, you want to start by defining what cognitive distortions are and maybe even give some examples to make it make sense. You can find a reference list of distortions on the following client-facing worksheet for this skill. Once the client has a baseline understanding of cognitive distortions, you can move forward by normalizing these types of thoughts—reminding them that everyone engages in them to some degree. Cognitive distortions are a very human way our brains try to protect us. They're wildly unhelpful most of the time, but at the end of the day, it's the brain being a brain, trying to keep us safe and survive. I like to explain it this way: "Our brains are storytellers. Sometimes they tell true stories, sometimes they tell scary, exaggerated ones. And here's the kicker—we don't have to believe every single story our minds tell!" You can use real-world or playful examples to illustrate, such as:

- Catastrophizing: "My friend hasn't texted back in two hours, so they probably hate me."
- All-or-nothing thinking: "If I don't ace this presentation, I'm a total failure."

At this point in the conversation, you can gently and nonjudgmentally highlight one or two distortions that seem to fit the client's patterns. For example, "I notice that sometimes you fall into some black-and-white thinking patterns. Do you feel like that's accurate?"

Addressing Common Client Pitfalls

Clients don't always greet the idea of cognitive distortions with open arms, and that's okay! Here are some common pushbacks you might hear, along with supportive ways to respond:

- **Clients say, "Yeah, but everyone thinks like this."**
  - → Respond with: "Totally. These are human habits. But noticing them gives us more power over how much they run the show."
- **Clients say, "Catching distortions just makes me feel worse, like I'm broken."**
  - → Respond with: "Actually, catching them is a real sign of strength. It means you're stepping back and observing your mind instead of being swept away by it, right?"
- **Clients say, "But what if my distortion is true?"**
  - → Respond with: "Good question and solid point. Sometimes our thoughts have a grain of truth, but distortions exaggerate or oversimplify. The goal isn't to erase the thought as much as it is to notice when your brain is adding extra drama that makes things feel worse than they are. If there is an area you feel needs improving, that's okay and we can work toward improving that—and at the same time [*dialectics*], you don't have to let your brain bully you into learning better strategies."
- **Clients say, "I don't know how to reframe."**
  - → Respond with: "That's okay, that's why we are here—to learn together! Sometimes I find that just labeling the distortion is a reframe in and of itself. Just clocking it is already half the battle. Over time, you'll get more comfortable softening the thought and trying out more balanced perspectives. If it helps, maybe reframe it in the same way you'd speak to someone you love and care about."

Final Notes

If you can, keep it light. Clients may feel ashamed when they start noticing their distorted thinking, so remember to normalize it as part of being human, because honestly, it is! And don't forget to remind them where you can: "You are not your thoughts. Thoughts are just mental events that come and go."

Client Worksheet

Cognitive Distortions

How to start recognizing unhelpful thinking patterns

Our brains can sometimes play tricks on us by telling stories that aren't fully true. These very annoying thinking habits are called *cognitive distortions*. They can make situations seem scarier, sadder, or more hopeless than they really are. The goal isn't to get rid of them (you're human, after all!) but to notice when they show up, gently reframe them, and ultimately lead yourself back to the present moment. Here are some common cognitive distortions:

All-or-nothing thinking: Seeing things in extremes, with no middle ground. This can show up in many different ways:

- ***Success or failure:*** Believing that anything less than perfect is a failure, not recognizing that progress and learning can be valuable outcomes.
- ***Good or bad people:*** Labeling someone as entirely good or bad based on one action or characteristic, without considering their complex traits and behaviors.
- ***Always or never:*** Assuming that someone will always or never do something based on a single instance or limited experience, without accounting for change or context.
- ***Love or hate:*** Believing that one can only feel complete love or hate for a person, place, or thing, rather than acknowledging mixed or evolving emotions.
- ***Right or wrong:*** Asserting that there is only one correct answer or approach to a situation or problem, not considering alternative perspectives or solutions.
- ***With me or against me:*** Assuming that if someone disagrees with a particular belief or opinion, they are completely opposed to you, rather than understanding that people can disagree on some issues and still share common ground.
- ***All or nothing:*** Believing that if a goal or task cannot be completed entirely or perfectly, it is not worth pursuing at all, instead of recognizing the value of partial accomplishments or gradual progress.
- ***Healthy or unhealthy:*** Believing that a single indulgence ruins an otherwise healthy diet, instead of recognizing that occasional treats can be part of a balanced lifestyle.
- ***Beautiful or ugly:*** Labeling something as either completely beautiful or completely ugly, not taking into account the subjective nature of beauty or appreciating the potential for mixed characteristics.
- ***Smart or stupid:*** Judging a person's intelligence based on one action or decision, without considering their knowledge, skills, and abilities in various areas.

Overgeneralization: Making sweeping conclusions based on one event.

- "I got one rejection, so I'll never succeed at anything."

Catastrophizing: Jumping straight to the worst-case scenario.

- "My friend is late and isn't answering her phone. She must have been in a car crash."

Personalization: Taking blame for things that are totally outside of your control.

- "My friend canceled plans. It must be because I'm boring and don't have much to offer in conversation."

Jumping to conclusions: Making negative assumptions without enough evidence. It can show up in two different ways:

- ***Mind-reading:*** Assuming you know what others think.
  - "She didn't smile, so she must hate me."
- ***Fortune-telling:*** Predicting a negative outcome.
  - "This conversation won't go well."

Mental filtering: Focusing only on the negatives and ignoring the potential positives.

- "I got mostly good feedback, but one critique means I've failed and I'm not doing well."

Discounting the positive: Downplaying good things that happen.

- "They said they liked me, but they were just being nice."

Should statements: Holding rigid rules about how things "should," "must" or "ought to" be.

- "I should never make mistakes."
- "I shouldn't feel emotional over this."

Emotional reasoning: Believing that feelings = facts.

- "Because I am feeling anxious, something bad must be happening."

Labeling: Attaching a negative, global label to yourself or others based on one mistake or one incident.

- "I messed up this presentation, so obviously I'm a failure."

Comparing/grass is greener: Believing others' lives are always better.

- "Everyone else is happier than me."
- "Everyone on social media has more friends than I do."

Now that you've learned some cognitive distortions and what they look like, let's practice noticing them in your own thinking.

What was a recent thought you had that felt really strong or upsetting?

Which distortion might this thought fit into?

How could you reframe it to be a more balanced or realistic thought?

What are the cognitive distortions you lean into most?

What might those cognitive distortions be trying to protect you from?

Pocket Mindfulness

Small, effective practices for staying present in real life

Mindfulness is often misunderstood as something that has to look a certain way: eyes closed, sitting still, deep in meditation. For many clients, that idea feels overwhelming, unrealistic, or even impossible. Sometimes it can feel that way even for us as clinicians!

Pocket mindfulness skills break down that barrier. They are these small, practical practices that a client can fit in their back pocket (literally or figuratively) and pull out whenever stress or distraction hits—or simply when they want to savor the moment. (Because don't forget, mindfulness is not just about slowing it down in tough times; it's also about saving the good stuff as well.) These skills make mindfulness approachable and less intimidating, while reinforcing the idea that mindfulness doesn't always mean sitting in silence for twenty minutes—it can be woven into everyday moments!

These bite-sized skills help clients build the muscle of attention. They're less about achieving some perfect Zen state and more about noticing the present moment, even in playful ways. That shift of noticing, describing, and engaging with what's right in front of them really is the essence of mindfulness. Over time, these little moments add up, making it easier for clients to stay present and regulate emotions when they need.

You can introduce the concept by saying something like:

"I know sometimes mindfulness can feel intimidating, but it doesn't have to be. It doesn't have to mean meditating on a cushion or transforming yourself into a Buddhist monk. It can be as simple as noticing the feel of your dog's fur while you pet them or paying attention to your food while you eat. Pocket mindfulness skills are quick, easy ways to come back to the moment, or even just slow things down a tad."

I encourage you to actually do the exercises on the accompanying client-facing worksheet in real time with the client because the best way to learn is to *do*! It also helps model the skills in session. Try to keep it light and playful so the client experiences mindfulness as something accessible, not rigid. I would also give them the disclaimer that some of these skills might seem silly or stupid at first, but they still pull us into the moment—regardless of how dumb they sound.

Addressing Common Client Pitfalls

Sometimes clients still don't buy into the concept of mindfulness. It can feel boring, silly, or like one more thing on their to-do list. Here are some common pushbacks you might hear and how you can respond:

- **Clients say, "I don't have time for mindfulness."**
  - → Respond with: "I totally hear that, and these skills are designed to take less than five minutes, some even less than one. Think of them like mental snacks instead of a full meal."

- **Clients say, "Mindfulness is boring."**
  - → Respond with: "Let's find a version that's fun for you then! Mindfulness is flexible, and we can adapt it to you. You don't have to adapt to it. I know you love music, so want to try mindful listening together and see if we can pick out and stay with the bass the whole song through?"
- **Clients say, "I feel silly doing these."**
  - → Respond with: "Totally fair. It can feel cringey to do at first! But the silliness is part of what makes them stick, and it honestly can be a part of the fun if you let it be. You also don't need to be super sophisticated in the skills for them to work. Think of it like exercising: It feels awkward the first time, but it strengthens your brain's ability to stay present."
- **Clients say, "What's the point of doing these small things?"**
  - → Respond with: "I hear you, and these can feel pointless, but every rep of mindfulness builds the habit for you. Just like lifting light weights over time builds strength, these small practices train your brain to stay calmer and more focused when bigger stressors hit. It also trains you to be in the here and now when things are good so you can find the present to be more fulfilling over time!"

Final Notes

Encourage clients to experiment with these skills throughout their day; while commuting, eating, and walking; or during small breaks. Emphasize that mindfulness is not about perfection but about practice. The more they use pocket skills, the more accessible mindfulness becomes in moments of distress! I have many clients who love these skills so much that we do them every session, either at the beginning to ground and prep them for session time, or toward the end for thoughtful containment. Have fun with it, be flexible, and lean into the simplicity of these skills.

Pocket Mindfulness

Small, effective practices for staying present in real life

Mindfulness doesn't have to mean sitting still for a long meditation. It can be flexible, fun, and easily accessible! Pocket mindfulness skills are short, simple practices you can use anytime, anywhere to bring yourself back to the present. Try them out and see which ones fit you best!

- **Celeb name game (or any list game):** Pick a category: celebs, dog breeds, foods, states—whatever you have an interest in! Take turns naming items in the category. Each new name must start with the last letter of the one before (e.g., Britney Spears → Sam Smith → Hannah Montana). This keeps your brain focused on one thing in the moment.
- **Mindful eating:** Slow down with a snack or meal. Notice the colors, textures, smells, tastes, and even the sounds of your food. Try describing the food as if you were trying to tell someone who has no idea what the food is all about it. Use as many descriptors as possible, taking your time. No rush!
- **Focus on one object:** Choose an object around you (e.g., pen, shoe, coffee mug—anything that's in the room with you) and describe it in detail using as many senses and descriptors as possible! Go until you can't anymore.
- **Band of light / muscle relaxation:** Imagine a gentle band of light moving slowly from the top of your head to your feet. As it moves, notice each body part. If you want, tense and release muscles along the way.
- **Five senses check-in:** Pause and notice: five things you see, four things you feel, three things you hear, two things you smell, and one thing you taste, right now.
- **Three minutes of writing:** Set a timer for three minutes and write whatever comes into your head. Don't edit—just let the thoughts flow. It doesn't have to be neat or in any particular format, and it doesn't even need to be legible or use real words. It can be whatever is in your mind at the moment.
- **Coloring or drawing:** Grab pens, crayons, or markers. Focus on the movement of your hand, the colors on the page, and the sound of the pen.
- **Mindful walk or movement:** Take a short walk. Pay attention to your steps, your breathing, and what you notice around you with all five senses.
- **Mindful listening:** Pick a song you love. For the whole song, just listen. Notice the instruments, rhythm, lyrics, and how it makes you feel.

Now that you've learned some pocket skills, brainstorm how to incorporate these skills into your routine.

Which pocket skill do you want to try first?

Where in your day could you fit it in? (Examples: commute, mealtime, break, bedtime)

After trying it, how did it feel?

MODULE 2

Distress Tolerance

Distress Tolerance: The Quick and Dirty

Distress tolerance is pretty much exactly what it sounds like: learning how to tolerate—you guessed it—distress! I like to define it as getting through a tough moment without making things worse. That's it. It's about surviving the shitstorm without doing something that leads to regret, shame, or long-term consequences once the moment passes. It's also important to note that these skills are not about feeling calm, happy, or Zen. It's called distress *tolerance*, after all—not distress elimination!

So what does distress actually do to us, physically and mentally?

When we're in distress, the nervous system goes into overdrive, specifically the sympathetic nervous system. And when we want relief *now*, we tend to reach for whatever gets us out of pain the fastest, whether it's shutting down, drinking, picking a fight, impulsively texting an ex, doom scrolling, spending money we shouldn't, or bingeing out on food. You name it. These short-term fixes provide relief in the moment, but they often create bigger messes for us to clean up later.

Distress tolerance skills give us a road map for navigating these moments safely, skillfully, and with our self-respect intact. They build a bridge between Emotional Mind and Wise Mind—a place where clients can tolerate discomfort without acting on it. And that's huge. Because when someone learns that they can survive distress without falling apart or numbing out, they start to trust themselves more. That's the magical part of this module. Clients learn the art of riding the wave instead of drowning in it.

These skills fall into four main areas in DBT:

1. **Distraction:** How can I get out of my head?
2. **Self-soothe:** How can I make my body more comfortable?
3. **Pros and cons:** What will be helpful about acting on my urges, and what will be unhelpful?
4. **Improving the moment:** Is there anything about this distress I can use to my advantage?

Distress Tolerance vs. Avoidance

Distress tolerance and avoidance can look almost identical to the untrained eye. Both can involve stepping away, taking a break, or distracting ourselves. The difference lies in the *intention*.

Distress tolerance is about managing the pain without running from it. It's a conscious, temporary pause that says, "This moment is too intense for me to problem-solve right now, so I'm going to use a skill to get through it until I can think clearly again." It's active coping. There's an awareness that the emotion will still be there later, and that's okay.

Avoidance, on the other hand, is an escape hatch. It's that instinct to check out completely and pretend the problem doesn't even exist. Avoidance feels like relief in the short term but robs clients of the chance to learn that they can handle discomfort, not to mention learn the skills to cope with difficult moments in life. It's like putting duct tape over a leaking pipe—it buys time, but the water's still coming.

In this module, the goal is to teach clients to tolerate distress, not to make it disappear entirely. That means helping them know when to lean into the emotion versus when to use a temporary distraction technique if leaning into the emotion isn't safe or possible in the moment. These skills are not for every bad mood or inconvenience. They're for moments when emotions are so high that logic has left the chat. Clients are not trying to fix their lives with these skills; they're just trying to get through the next hour safely. Distress tolerance helps them ride the wave until it settles. Avoidance keeps them from ever getting in the water.

Distress tolerance builds resilience, while avoidance builds dependence. Our job as clinicians is to help clients spot that difference because, often, avoidance can be sneaky. It likes to dress up as "self-care," "space," or "rest," but if you're not returning to the underlying issue at some point, then it's, as the kids would say, "not the vibe."

How to Explain Distress Tolerance So Clients Actually Want to Use It

If you tell a client that distress tolerance means "accepting reality as it is," you'll probably lose them by the second word. Most people don't walk into therapy wanting to "tolerate" anything. That's a drag. They want to feel better. The trick is explaining this module in a way that's relatable, not theoretical. You might say, "Distress tolerance doesn't mean you have to like what's happening or that you're okay with it. It simply means you're learning how to get through it without making things worse. You're enduring. You're tolerating." That line usually lands because it speaks directly to the client's lived experience. Everyone knows what it's like to make a bad situation worse by reacting impulsively. We can all connect to that!

I also like to frame distress tolerance as emotional first aid kit. When you break a bone, you don't try to run a marathon that day—you stabilize it so it can heal properly. These skills are kind of the emotional equivalent of a splint. They're not about solving the problem; they're about keeping the damage from spreading until you're in a calmer state and can think clearly again. It's the splint, not the surgery.

When in doubt, make it concrete by asking the client what they usually do when they're overwhelmed. Most clients will list coping habits that give quick relief but long-term pain, like numbing, lashing out, isolating, drinking, scrolling, or spending. That's your opening. Here, you can say, "Distress tolerance helps you build new versions of those same coping habits, but without the aftermath!" Clients don't have to love these skills; they just have to use them long enough to get through the wave. And because they're built for the moment, they are great to reinforce via phone coaching as well.

The SUDs Scale

In this module, you don't just ask clients to use skills and blindly hope that they'll feel better. No way. You measure. You track. You get data.

That's where the SUDs scale comes in. SUDs stands for *subjective units of distress*—literally meaning, how distressed are you? Everyone anchors this scale a little differently, but I like to keep it simple with a 0–10 scale, with 0 being the lowest intensity of an urge or an emotion that someone can feel, and 10 being the highest. Clients use this scale to monitor where they are at any given point when experiencing distress, and to track which skills help bring them down on the scale.

With the SUDs scale, there's also something called the TLA, or *tolerable level of arousal.* Think of it as the zone on the SUDs scale where a person can be emotionally charged yet still stay present, notice what's happening in their body, and think clearly enough to choose a skillful response. It's the emotional range where the prefrontal cortex is still online and the amygdala hasn't completely left the room.

Most people function best when their arousal level hangs somewhere between a 3 and a 7 or 8. Below a 3, they're usually not distressed. They're just checked out or bored (unless they're on a beach chair in the sun, in which case their nervous system gets a free pass). But sitting in that low-arousal zone for long stretches, especially when they have no choice in the matter, can feel emotionally numbing for some clients.

Once a person climbs past their TLA, somewhere above a 7 or so, the brain starts to get overwhelmed. This is where clients slip into emotional flooding. *Flooding* is that awful place where emotions feel huge, fast, and consuming, like getting hit by a wave you never saw coming. People often describe it as drowning in their own feelings. They can't remember what it felt like to be calm, and they doubt they'll ever get back there. It's the *Titanic* moment when Jack and Rose are caught by the locked gate and the water is rising quickly.

When someone shoots past their TLA, they usually fall into one of five predictable coping patterns. It's helpful to identify what a client's typical pattern is so you can better point it out when it's happening in real time:

1. **Top-down management:** This is the client who shuts out their emotions entirely, goes numb, and retreats into pure logic. In an actual emergency, this can be useful, but as a long-term strategy, it disconnects people from their bodies and makes it impossible to process feelings later. It's Rational Mind on steroids.

2. **Emotional takeover:** This is classic Emotional Mind—seeing red, spiraling into a panic attack, or feeling hit with a wave of emotionality so intense it temporarily wipes out clear thinking. The more intense the emotion, the less access clients have to reasoning, which is why saying "calm down" never works here.

3. **Circular thinking:** Clients stuck in this loop are thinking, but not effectively. Thoughts go around and around like a hamster wheel. They're trying to solve a problem with a brain that is way outside its TLA, so problem-solving is basically offline. Think of someone who has just been through a trauma saying, "This can't be happening" over and over again. It's the brain trying to work through something that is extremely overwhelming but doing so unsuccessfully.
4. **Agitation:** This can show up as literal pacing, restlessness, or an internal buzzing energy that won't settle. It's the nervous system flooded with adrenaline and trying to release it but without any real direction.
5. **Dissociation:** Clients may zone out for a few seconds, feel like they're watching their lives from the outside, or lose complete track of time. It's the nervous system's emergency eject button when things feel too overwhelming to stay fully present.

Once clients can understand what it looks like when they're outside their TLA, the purpose of these skills becomes clearer. While these skills won't magically fix the situation, they do get people back into a range where their brain can function again. And once clients realize that their nervous system has an actual "sweet spot," they become much more motivated to use skills that bring their SUDs down quickly instead of relying on strategies that keep them stuck or make things worse.

Pocket Distress Tolerance

A quick calm-down toolkit

When it comes to pocket distress tolerance, we're talking about survival or crisis skills that clients can use when they're past their TLA. These are the quick hitters—the skills clients can use when their SUDs level shoots up fast, their brain goes offline, and they need something that works *right now*. These skills engage the body, not the mind, because once a client is outside their TLA, nobody is reasoning their way out of anything. Pocket skills help bring the nervous system back within an optimal zone so clients can think, problem-solve, and not act on impulse.

Let's break down the big three: TIPP, STOP, and ACCEPTS.

TIPP: Changing Your Body to Change Your Brain

TIPP is the go-to skill when emotions feel too big for the moment. The whole goal is to shift physiology fast enough so the brain can reset. Clients can use one of these, all of them, or a mix of those that work. Whatever they prefer! TIPP is the best when they are past their TLA and just need a quick grounding skill. Let's break down the components.

- **Temperature:** Cold exposure triggers something called the "dive response." It's a built-in survival reflex humans share with seals and penguins, which is honestly kind of adorable. When the face or body hits cold water, heart rate drops, blood vessels tighten, and oxygen is conserved. It's the body's way of saying, "Hey, let's not die right now!" Clients often describe the effect as grounding, steadying, or a mental reset. This is why cold plunges, cold showers, splashing cold water on the face, or even holding a frozen ice pack can be so calming.
- **Intense movement:** Ever notice how some people swear the gym is their therapy? That's the I in TIPP. When emotions flood the system, intense movement gives the body somewhere to put all that energy. It burns off cortisol and adrenaline, which are the stress chemicals that build up when the nervous system goes into high alert. Using them up through movement helps bring the body back down to baseline. On top of that, intense movement releases endorphins, dopamine, and serotonin. It also cuts through rumination because the brain has to focus on breathing and moving. A run, boxing class, fast walk, dance break, or even 100 jumping jacks can interrupt emotional escalation and help reset the nervous system.
- **Paced breathing:** Slow, steady breaths activate the parasympathetic nervous system, the part of the body that says we're safe and can settle. It increases oxygen flow, relaxes muscles, and shifts attention away from spiraling thoughts. A simple fivefold breath works beautifully: inhale for five, hold for five, exhale for five, hold for five, repeat. Even one minute of this can take the edge off a wave of distress.
- **Paired muscle relaxation:** Progressive muscle relaxation helps clients release the physical tension that often goes hand in hand with anxiety. It involves tensing a muscle group,

holding for a few seconds, releasing, and then noticing the change. This not only reduces physical tension but increases awareness of body cues and gives people a sense of control when emotions feel loud or messy. It's grounding, simple, and incredibly effective.

STOP: The Pause Button for Your Nervous System

STOP is the skill that prevents people from making the moment worse. It gives clients a beat between the urge and the action, which in DBT is half the battle. It's fantastic for folks who struggle a lot with impulsivity. Let's break down the components.

- **Stop:** Freeze the impulse. Do nothing. Don't act on what Emotional Mind wants to do. This is the skill that saves people from the text they will absolutely regret. I literally tell clients (and myself) to do nothing. Don't move, don't breathe, don't talk. Literally stop. If it helps, ask clients to picture a big bright red stop sign in front of their face.
- **Take a step back:** Step back physically or mentally. Take a breath, create a moment of space, or take a quick walk to the hallway. Distance gives the brain just enough room to start coming down from the surge.
- **Observe:** This involves pausing and asking, "What's happening right now in my body? My thoughts? The environment?" This gets clients out of autopilot and back into awareness. This is the same as the observe skill in the mindfulness module. Consider it an internal inventory of the moment.
- **Proceed mindfully:** Here, clients act with their goals in mind rather than their urges. Some questions to ask in the moment: "What am I working on in therapy right now? What will make this situation better? What will definitely make this worse? Is this action something I will be proud of later?" It's the reset button that keeps crises from escalating.

And lastly . . .

ACCEPTS: A Menu of Healthy Distractions

ACCEPTS is the Swiss army knife of distress tolerance. It's a list of distraction strategies clients can pull from when they need something to occupy their minds while their emotions cool down. The goal isn't to avoid the emotion forever. It's to give the nervous system time to settle so clients can return to the problem with clarity.

And here's the thing that really matters: An ACCEPTS list has to be specific and personal. Generic answers like "Watch TV" or "Listen to music" won't cut it when someone is overwhelmed. In those moments, the brain needs something that genuinely grabs attention and pulls focus away from the distress. I always tell clients, "Don't make more work for your future distressed self. Do that work now."

So instead of "Watch TV," a better option would be "Watch the new episode of *The Office* I've been waiting for." Instead of "Listen to music," clients can try "Listen to my 2013 nostalgia playlist." The more specific, the better. Have fun with it too! There are zero rules here. If a client loves a good pimple-popping video, put it on their list! When clients choose things they actually want to do, the skill works ten times better in real moments of distress.

Let's break down the components.

- **Activities:** Engage in anything that fully engages the client's attention: watching a show they're actually excited about, going for a walk, cleaning a specific part of the home, baking something, calling a friend, doing a puzzle. The key is choosing something that pulls them in.
- **Contributing:** Do something helpful or kind for someone else: donate clothes, help a friend with a project, send someone an encouraging message, offer a small kindness. Even tiny acts of contribution can shift emotional intensity.
- **Comparing:** Put the current moment in perspective. How does this situation compare to past challenges the client has survived? What strengths did they use then? What's different now? Comparison isn't about minimizing pain. It's about grounding in perspective.
- **Emotions:** Create a different emotion to interrupt the current one: watch a funny clip, listen to a powerful song, put on a comfort show, read something tender or inspiring, or watch something scary to shift the emotional channel. Anything that evokes a different feeling!
- **Push away:** Temporarily set the distress aside so the nervous system can recover. Say, "I'm not thinking about this for ten minutes." Step outside for air. Get a coffee. Physically leave the environment if that's what's needed. It's a pause, not avoidance. It's sort of similar to a worry window!
- **Thoughts:** Engage the brain in something structured, whether that's crossword puzzles, mental games, listening to a thought-provoking podcast, reciting lyrics, naming as many NYC subway stops as possible, doing math equations, or learning a new language. Anything that pulls cognition away from the distress cycle.
- **Sensations:** Use physical sensations to ground or distract, such as soaking in a warm bath, taking a cold shower, holding an ice pack, using scented lotion, playing with texture, squeezing a stress ball, or feeling the weight of a blanket. Sensory input can interrupt emotional overload quickly.

Pocket Distress Tolerance

A quick calm-down toolkit

These skills are designed for the moments when your emotions feel too big, too fast, or too overwhelming. When you notice you're above your *tolerable level of arousal* (your TLA), these skills help bring your mind and body back into a calmer zone so you can think clearly and make choices you'll feel good about. Use this worksheet to create your own personal pocket distress tolerance plan.

TIPP: Change Your Body to Change Your Brain

Temperature

What cold item can you use to calm your body quickly? (Examples: hold an ice pack, splash cold water on your face, hold a bag of frozen veggies, take a cold shower)

____

____

Intense Movement

Pick movement or a form of exercise that burns off adrenaline and gets your body moving. (Examples: sprinting, jumping jacks, push-ups, cycling, boxing)

____

____

Paced Breathing

Try taking slow, steady breaths. Which breathing exercise calms you down? (Examples: fivefold breath [inhale 5, hold 5, exhale 5, hold 5], 4-7-8 breathing, box breathing)

____

____

Paired Muscle Relaxation

Pick one muscle group at a time, tense it for a few seconds, then release and notice the difference. Which muscle groups will you focus on when you need to release tension?

____

____

STOP: Hit Pause Before You React

Stop

When you feel the urge to react, literally pause your body. Freeze and do nothing for a few seconds. What situations tend to trigger your biggest urges? What will remind you to stop in those moments?

____

____

Take a Step Back

After you pause, create space. Step into another room or mentally remove yourself from the situation. Where can you go (or what can you do) to create a little space when emotions run high?

____

____

Observe

Take inventory of what's happening in your body, emotions, and thoughts. What physical and emotional cues tell you that you're becoming overwhelmed?

____

____

Proceed Mindfully

Choose your next step intentionally. Ask yourself what outcome you actually want. What will make this situation better and what will make it worse? What action will you be proud of later?

____

____

ACCEPTS: Your Personalized Distraction Menu

Activities

What activities fully pull your attention in? Choose things that truly absorb your attention and be specific. Instead of saying "Watch TV," name exactly what movie or show you'll watch.

____

____

Contributing

Small acts of kindness can shift your focus outward and reduce distress. What is one concrete way you can contribute (even in a small way) to help someone else?

___

___

Comparing

Emotions can often make things feel bigger than they are. Remind yourself of past challenges you've survived. What past experiences remind you that you can handle difficult emotions?

___

___

Emotions

Do something that changes your mood, whether it's watching a funny video or listening to upbeat music. What can reliably create a different emotion for you?

___

___

Push Away

Give your nervous system a break by pushing away the situation for a while. This isn't about avoiding it forever, just setting it aside for the moment. How can you temporarily set the distress aside?

___

___

Thoughts

Engage your mind to stop yourself from spiraling. You might count backward, do a memory game, or solve a puzzle. What thought-based distractions work for you?

___

___

Sensations

Use strong sensory input to give yourself a reset, whether it's using scented lotion, taking a hot shower, or sucking on sour candy. What sensory experiences calm or ground you?

___

___

Your Pocket Distress Tolerance Plan

When you notice that you're overwhelmed (above your TLA), what TIPP, STOP, or ACCEPTS skills will you try first?

If those don't work, what skills will you try next?

Where will you keep this list so you can use it easily? (Examples: Notes app on your phone, wallet)

Five Senses Grounding

Grounding through the body

Self-soothe is one of those deceptively simple skills that can make a massive impact when clients are overwhelmed. The goal is to use the senses to help the body settle enough to bring the thinking brain back online. Clients often try to "logic" their way out of distress, which is adorable but wildly ineffective when the nervous system is in full fight-or-flight mode. Self-soothe bypasses all that by working directly through sensory input.

I usually frame this skill by asking clients to imagine how they'd take care of a scared child. They wouldn't give that child a TED Talk. They'd wrap them in a cozy blanket, put on their favorite movie, hand them something warm to drink, and sit close by until the child settled. Self-soothe involves learning to give themselves that same comfort when their system is overwhelmed. And specificity is everything here! "Watch something calming" is vague and forgettable. "Watch *Planet Earth* with a fuzzy blanket and a cup of sleepy time tea" is a self-soothe plan. The more personal and detailed their list is, the more likely they'll actually use it!

To teach this skill, start by explaining that sensory experiences directly activate the parasympathetic nervous system. That means touching, smelling, tasting, or hearing something calming can soothe the body faster than a two-hour TED Talk ever could. When clients are dysregulated, you don't want them talking, analyzing, or thinking their way out of the moment. You want them anchoring into the senses.

In DBT, we traditionally use the five senses, but we also treat movement as a sixth sense because for many clients, their bodies regulate best through motion. Think of it as "kinesthetic soothing," especially for folks who get more activated when they sit still. Movement can look gentle (e.g., stretching, rocking, slow walking) or more energizing (e.g., dance breaks, gym stair master, pacing). It's just as valid as any other sensory input, and for some clients it becomes one of their strongest tools!

How to Make a Self-Soothe List

Go through each of the six senses with your client, one at a time, and ask them specifically what comforts them when they are overwhelmed. For sight, you might ask something like "What can you look at that might be calming for you?" Some examples could be nature documentaries, calming cooking TikToks, or their favorite nostalgic show (shout-out to *Gilmore Girls*!). Encourage clients to think of extremely personalized, concrete examples that matter to them. If they write "music," ask "Which exact songs?" If they write "comfort food," ask "Which one? What flavor?" No vagueness allowed. The more precise, the more effective!

Once their list is done, encourage them to keep it somewhere they'll actually remember. And remind them that self-soothing is not avoidance or immaturity—it's nervous system care, plain and simple. If you want to take it one step further, it can be fun to encourage clients to create their own on-the-go senses pack so soothing stimuli is always within reach. They can go to Target or the Dollar Store, pick up a cute little fanny pack of sorts, go through the five senses, and put items in their fanny pack that soothe them. Think a little fidget toy, a small bottle of essential oils, a physical picture of loved ones, some sour candies, and whatever else is soothing to the five senses!

Five Senses Grounding

Grounding through the body

Self-soothing is all about using your senses to bring your body and mind back into a calmer state. When you are overwhelmed, it can be hard to think your way out of the moment. Your senses help you settle enough to ride the wave without making things worse.

In DBT, we use six categories: sight, hearing, taste, touch, smell, and movement. The goal is to fill in each section with specific things that actually soothe you. When you notice your distress rising, pick one or two items from your list and try them. The goal is not to erase the emotion. The goal is to soothe your body enough that the emotion becomes more tolerable. You can add to this list anytime. The more personal and detailed you make it, the more helpful it will be when you need it.

Sight

What are comforting or calming things you can look at?

Examples: Watch a sunrise or sunset, look at old photos that bring joy, watch a comfort show you've seen a million times, look at calming nature videos (e.g., rain, ocean waves), organize or tidy a small space, look at soft lighting like candles or string lights

___

___

___

Hearing

What sounds, music, voices, or audio help you settle?

Examples: Listen to your favorite playlist, play white noise or rain sounds, listen to a podcast that feels comforting or familiar, hear a loved one's voice note, play instrumental or lo-fi music, sit in silence if that feels grounding

___

___

___

Taste

What flavors, snacks, drinks, or comfort foods soothe your body?

Examples: Sip a warm drink like tea or coffee, eat something crunchy (e.g., chips, carrots, pretzels), slowly savor a piece of chocolate, chew gum or a mint, have a favorite comfort meal, drink something cold and refreshing

Touch

What textures, sensations, or physical comforts help your body feel safer?

Examples: Wrap up in a soft blanket, take a warm shower, hold something cold like an ice pack, pet an animal, wear cozy clothes, squeeze a stress ball or fidget, put on lotion and massage your hands

Smell

What scents help you relax, feel grounded, or feel comforted?

Examples: Light a candle, use essential oils (e.g., lavender, eucalyptus), smell fresh laundry, spray a favorite perfume, smell coffee brewing, step outside for fresh air

Movement

What kinds of movement help your nervous system settle? These can be gentle or energizing.

Examples: Go for a walk, stretch your body, do gentle yoga, pace around the room, dance to music, shake out your hands and arms, do a quick workout (or even just a few jumping jacks)

Pros and Cons

A reality check for your urges

The pros and cons skill is one of DBT's core distress tolerance strategies, designed for moments when clients feel the urge to do something that might make things worse. When emotions are running high, people often operate from emotion-driven behavior rather than thoughtful decision-making. The brain goes into "fix this feeling right now" mode, long-term consequences be damned. Pros and cons bring the thinking brain back online.

In particular, this skill helps clients slow down and think through the potential outcomes of an urge before acting on it. It encourages them to pause, weigh their options, and consider both the short-term and long-term consequences of their choices. Rather than focusing only on the urge itself, this skill is unique in that it invites clients to step back and evaluate two possibilities:

1. What are the pros and cons of acting on the urge?
2. What are the pros and cons of resisting the urge and using skills instead?

It is especially helpful when clients are feeling overwhelmed by intense emotions and are tempted to engage in impulsive or self-destructive behaviors. Sometimes just taking a beat and playing the tape forward can make a huge difference for someone who tends to lean into their impulsivity and then pays the price later. This exercise helps clients see that while emotion-driven behaviors may provide immediate relief, they unfortunately also often come with significant long-term costs. At the same time, choosing skillful behavior may feel harder in the moment but tends to support the life they ultimately want to build. We want to honor the fact that choosing skills, although the objectively healthy option, can feel like a con to some if it means they have to sit in more discomfort!

To teach this skill in session, I like to start by explaining that when emotions spike, we tend to zoom in on short-term relief and ignore the bigger picture. It feels like our brains are on fire, and we are ready and willing to do anything to put it out. Pros and cons help widen the lens. You might explain it by saying something like "When an urge hits, it can feel incredibly convincing, almost like your brain is saying, 'This is the only way to make this feeling stop!' The pros and cons skill helps you pause and ask, 'Okay, but what actually happens if I do this . . . and what actually happens if I don't?'"

Next, walk the client through a real example they're currently struggling with. Encourage them to write down the following:

- **Pros of acting on the urge:** What might feel good, relieving, or satisfying in the moment? What makes the urge appealing right now?
- **Cons of acting on the urge:** What problems could this create for them later? Think about short-term and long-term effects on their relationships, goals, self-respect, or well-being.

- **Pros of resisting the urge and using skills instead:** What might be better for them in the long run if they don't act on the urge? How could using a skill protect their goals, relationships, or sense of self?
- **Cons of resisting the urge and using skills instead:** What might feel difficult, uncomfortable, or frustrating about not giving in to the urge right now?

It's important to validate that some urges truly do have short-term benefits. I find that if we only condemn maladaptive urges, it can feel a bit invalidating because these actions have actually helped the client survive crises in the past. For example, yelling during an argument might release tension and avoiding a difficult situation might temporarily reduce anxiety. Acknowledging these short-term rewards keeps the skill honest and authentic, allowing clients to engage with the process rather than feeling lectured at.

Once you validate that some of these urges *do* have some real short-term benefits, you want to gently guide the client toward the bigger picture—helping them recognize that the short-term relief of acting on an urge comes at the expense of long-term goals, such as healthier relationships, emotional stability, and self-respect. In this way, the urge is likely to hinder them more than it helps them.

Pro tip: This skill works best before or during an urge, not after the behavior has already happened. You might even encourage clients to keep a written pros and cons list on their phone or somewhere visible so they can revisit it when urges show up.

If you want to take it one step further, it can also be helpful to focus especially on the long-term pros of skillful behavior and the long-term cons of impulsive behavior since those are the pieces clients tend to overlook when emotions are intense. You can even frame it this way: "When we're distressed, our brains are very persuasive about why the urge makes sense. Pros and cons help us become a little less reactive and a little more intentional."

Over time, practicing this skill helps clients strengthen the pause between urge and action, which is one of the most important muscles we're building in DBT.

Pros and Cons

A reality check for your urges

When emotions and distress are running high, it might seem like acting on an urge—sending an angry text, avoiding something important, using substances, shutting down—is the only way to get relief. The challenge is that your brain tends to focus on what will make you feel better *right now* while ignoring the bigger picture and longer-term consequences.

The pros and cons skill can help you slow things down and take a step back before reacting. Think of it as a "check yourself before you wreck yourself" skill. Instead of automatically following through with the urge, you want to pause and look at the potential consequences of your choices.

This exercise will help you explore:

- What might feel good about acting on the urge
- What problems it might create later
- What could happen if you resist the urge and use skills instead

There are no right or wrong answers here. The goal is simply to give your brain a chance to think things through before the urge takes over.

What's the Urge?

Think about a situation where you're feeling a strong urge to do something that might make things worse. What is the urge you are experiencing right now?

____

The Pros of Acting on the Urge

What might feel good, relieving, or satisfying about acting on the urge? Even urges that lead to problems usually have something about them that feels appealing in the moment.

____

____

____

____

____

The Cons of Acting on the Urge

What problems could this create for you later? Think about short-term and long-term consequences. (Examples: damaged relationships, loss of trust, regret over impulsive actions, increased stress)

____

____

____

____

____

The Pros of Resisting the Urge and Using Skills Instead	The Cons of Resisting the Urge
What might be better in the long run if you don't act on the urge? (Examples: you might avoid unnecessary drama, you enhance your sense of self-worth, you feel proud of yourself, you create greater peace of mind)	What might feel difficult or uncomfortable about not giving in to the urge right now? (Examples: you have to wait for the situation to improve, you feel like you're giving up control, you struggle to sit with intense emotions, you feel like it's too hard to use skills)
____________________	____________________
____________________	____________________
____________________	____________________
____________________	____________________
____________________	____________________

Final Reflection

Looking at everything you wrote on this worksheet, what choice moves you closer to the kind of life you want to build?

____

____

____

What skill could help you get through this moment instead of acting on the urge?

____

____

____

Making Lemonade from Lemons

Making the best of a hard moment without pretending it's fine

Making lemonade is one of the more uplifting distress tolerance skills, but I've found that it's also one of the trickiest to teach well. This skill lives under the "IMPROVE the Moment" umbrella in distress tolerance and centers on making meaning from suffering. Not sugarcoating, not pretending things are fine, not forcing gratitude. It's about widening the lens of a difficult moment just enough to see what else might be true besides the pain.

Hear me out. This one can be a bit polarizing because some clients think this skill is the same as toxic positivity or that it invalidates their struggles, so it's important to clarify *very* early on that you are not asking them to deny what they're going through. And here's an important nuance I always point out: You've probably heard the phrase "Everything happens for a reason." While it sounds nice in theory, it can feel like a jagged pill to swallow, especially for clients who have gone through big-T traumas or losses that genuinely have no justifying "reason."

In DBT, we take a different stance. Instead of saying, "Everything happens for a reason," I like to say, "Things happen, and we can choose to make meaning from them." That wording protects clients from feeling blamed for their suffering while still giving them agency to create something helpful out of what happened. You're asking them to consider whether something helpful, clarifying, or growth-producing might come out of the pain, including the struggle itself. In DBT terms, it's the art of holding the truth of the hardship in one hand and the possibility of meaning in the other. Think Viktor Frankl's *A Man's Search for Meaning*.

I have found that this skill is best used when a client is in distress but not in crisis. If you try to introduce it during a crisis, you run the risk of it being received as very invalidating and even harmful. It's more so for moments where the emotions are painful yet manageable, and where a shift in perspective could actually help them move through the moment without spiraling further. Things like breakups, job loss, friendship drama, disappointing news, conflict with family, or even the sting of everyday annoyances are all perfect opportunities for this skill!

To teach this skill, start by validating that lemons are, in fact, sour! Clients need to feel seen before they can even begin to consider finding meaning in the moment. Once that's clear, you can introduce the idea that distress tolerance involves learning to ask, "Is there anything here that could help me grow, heal, understand, or shift something in my life?" while *also* holding the pain of the event. Humor can work beautifully here. You might say, "We're not turning your suffering into a Pinterest quote. We're just seeing if there's anything here that makes the moment feel less pointless."

Use concrete examples to ground this skill so it doesn't remain ambiguous. For instance, losing a job is painful, but it might also push someone toward a career that fits better. Being criticized might sting, but it can also highlight something that the person needs to work on changing. A fight with a partner might reveal needs that haven't been voiced yet. The key is not to pretend the situation is totally fine, but to see whether something good can come from it as well.

Self-disclosure moment: This can be a great opportunity to share an appropriate anecdote from your own life—a time when struggle led to a moment of growth.

Common Pitfalls and How to Address Them

Clients may feel pressured to "find the good" before they are ready. Normalize that not every lemon has immediate lemonade. For some moments, the meaning only shows up in hindsight. Encourage them to try the skill gently, not forcefully. If you've ever seen *This Is Us*, in the very first episode Jack talks about finding life's sourest lemon and making "something resembling" lemonade. So remember, this doesn't have to be a perfect process of finding earth-shattering meaning. It just needs to be something to make the struggle slightly worthwhile. In addition, don't jump into meaning-making too soon. If someone is deeply dysregulated, go with grounding or self-soothing skills first. The thinking brain has to come back online before it can start making lemonade.

The big therapeutic win here is helping clients see that even when they can't control a situation, they can create meaning from it. Meaning gives suffering direction. Direction gives suffering purpose. And purpose makes distress more tolerable.

Making Lemonade from Lemons

Making the best of a hard moment without pretending it's fine

Sometimes life hands us situations that are incredibly painful, disappointing, or just plain unfair. To be clear, this skill is not about pretending everything is fine or forcing positivity. It's about gently exploring whether any meaning, growth, or clarity can come from a tough moment. Instead of telling yourself, "Everything happens for a reason," which can feel really invalidating when you're in pain, this skill asks you to take a more compassionate perspective: "Things happen, and I can choose to make meaning from them." This can make the moment feel a little more tolerable, a little less pointless, and a little more connected to your values and growth.

Use this worksheet to help you look at your situation with curiosity instead of judgment. If this clarity only comes with time and retrospection, that's okay too. Be gentle on yourself. ☺

Step 1: What's the Lemon?

Describe the situation you are going through. What happened? What makes it painful or difficult?

____

____

____

Step 2: What Thoughts or Feelings Are Showing Up?

What exactly feels distressing here? Be honest and specific.

____

____

____

Step 3: Is There Any Lemonade Here?

Read the following questions and place a check mark on the ones that fit your situation. Not all will apply. You only need one small strand of meaning.

- ☐ Is this situation helping me see something more clearly?
- ☐ Is it teaching me something I didn't know?
- ☐ Is it giving me a chance to let go of something that has been weighing on me?
- ☐ Is it bringing me closer to someone?
- ☐ Is it preparing me for a change?
- ☐ Is it awakening creativity or personal strength?

- ☐ Is it showing me something about myself that I overlooked?
- ☐ Is it helping me practice patience, acceptance, or resilience?
- ☐ Is it revealing a boundary I didn't realize I needed?
- ☐ Is it reminding me of what actually matters to me?
- ☐ Is it giving me insight into what I want to do differently going forward?
- ☐ Is it reminding me I can survive moments I thought I couldn't?
- ☐ Is it helping me build compassion for myself or others?
- ☐ Is it nudging me toward a path I have been avoiding?
- ☐ Is it challenging beliefs or stories I've been holding on to?
- ☐ Is it showing me where I need connection or support?
- ☐ Is it helping me notice that this feeling is temporary?
- ☐ Is it pointing to something that needs healing?
- ☐ Is it helping me become more aligned with the version of myself I want to be?

Reflect on any meaningful threads that came up for you with this exercise.

____

____

____

Step 4: Putting It Together

What meaning are you choosing to make from this situation? Even a tiny shift counts!

____

____

____

Positive/Neutral Coping Thoughts

Choosing thoughts that help rather than escalate emotions

This skill is a quickie, but a goodie. On the surface, it might look like just saying helpful self-statements, but in reality, it's a form of cognitive distress tolerance and cognitive restructuring, which is way more powerful than most of us give it credit for. When someone is in a tough moment, the way they talk to themselves can either pour gasoline on the fire or help them survive the moment without making things worse. Positive/neutral coping thoughts give them a script for the latter.

This skill is essentially about helping your client become their own little cheerleader during a difficult time. They're not lying to themselves or forcing positivity—they are choosing thoughts that keep them steady enough to ride the wave when they're already in distress. When clients learn to talk to themselves in a way that is truthful and compassionate, they are practicing radical acceptance, emotion regulation, and distress tolerance all at once.

This skill is great for clients who tend to default to harsh self-criticism and need a structured way to practice a more compassionate tone. It's best used when:

- Clients are emotionally activated but still able to think.
- The situation cannot be changed immediately.
- Impulsive urges are rising.
- The client is catastrophizing or spiraling.
- Shame is loud and they need a counter-voice.

However, note that not every coping thought works for every person. If a statement doesn't resonate, it won't regulate. (You like that little rhyme there?) You want clients to choose phrases that genuinely feel like their voice and their truth. Picking random Pinterest quotes or saying things they don't believe usually backfires and creates more frustration. You want realistic, believable, specific thoughts that meet the moment as best as possible.

This is why the accompanying client-facing worksheet includes a wide range of styles, from gentle validation ("It's okay to have a not-okay day") to humor ("Not my monkeys, not my circus"), to boundary reminders ("I am not responsible for managing someone else's emotions"), to body-image neutrality ("We don't have to change to fit the clothes—the clothes can change to fit us"). The variety helps clients find statements that actually land.

How to Teach This Skill

Start by explaining that a distressed brain tends to generate distorted or catastrophic thoughts. Positive/neutral coping thoughts interrupt that spiral by offering a more grounded internal narrative. They help clients shift from Emotional Mind toward something closer to Wise Mind.

Next, help the client identify the harsh or negative thoughts they are telling themselves that are causing more distress. Then, introduce several positive/neutral coping thoughts that fit the client's specific situation. Feel free to look at the examples on the accompanying client-facing worksheet for guidance. For example, if they feel overwhelmed by visiting their parents for the holidays because of the emotional baggage it brings, perhaps they can look at coping thoughts that center around not carrying pain that isn't theirs. For this specific situation, I like to use "This emotion is not mine to hold," but come up with a few for good measure! Ask them to notice which phrases produce even a tiny bit of softening in the body. That's their nervous system signaling "This one works!"

Encourage clients to write their own phrases too. The blank lines on the worksheet are there for personalized mantras that feel like them. Perhaps they heard a line in a favorite song or remember a quote from an inspiring movie that they feel could fit here—add it! Humor can be a powerful tool here. Statements like "Shit happens sometimes" or "This person is difficult, but maybe my experience with them will help me learn something, like patience or empathy" can help clients loosen rigid thinking and make the process feel lighter.

Addressing Common Client Pitfalls

Positive/neutral coping thoughts will only help if clients pick phrases that work for them (and actually remember to use them!). Here are some of these common traps and how to avoid them:

- **Clients choose thoughts that sound good but don't feel true.**
  - → Reinforce the importance of phrases that *resonate* with the client. Statements like "Everything will work out" might sound good in session, but it may not actually help if the client genuinely doesn't believe it. Encourage them to find something that feels honest, such as "This is hard *and* I'm doing my best" or "I don't know how this will end, but I know I can get through today one moment at a time."
- **Clients confuse coping thoughts with denial or forced positivity.**
  - → Coping thoughts aren't about pretending. The goal is to give clients a compassionate internal narrator they can rely on in difficult moments. When they learn to access that voice, distress becomes more tolerable and impulsive behaviors decrease. It's about supporting themselves through the pain without adding suffering. Again, think gentle cheerleader.
- **Clients forget to use these statements when distressed.**
  - → Have clients prepare a go-to list of statements for recurring situations and rehearse them ahead of time to build muscle memory. They can also put these phrases on a phone widget or write them on sticky notes and place them where they can see them often—whatever works!

Positive/Neutral Coping Thoughts

Choosing thoughts that help rather than escalate emotions

When you are going through a tough moment, the way you talk to yourself truly matters! Positive or neutral coping thoughts help you get through the distress without making things worse.

To practice this skill, first be clear about what situation is currently causing you distress. Describe it in as much detail as you can.

____

____

____

____

____

____

____

____

Now, look through the following list and put a check mark by any of the statements that genuinely feel helpful to you. Not every one will fit! Only choose the ones that land.

- ☐ It's okay to have a not-okay day.
- ☐ Things could always be worse.
- ☐ Let them, and let me.
- ☐ I've dealt with harder situations, and I know it will get better.
- ☐ Shit happens sometimes. It just be like that sometimes.
- ☐ Progress isn't linear.
- ☐ Healing is a marathon, not a sprint.
- ☐ I don't have to be perfect. I'm human.
- ☐ I am not a perfect person, and I will make mistakes.
- ☐ I'm doing the best I can.
- ☐ I did the best I could with the skills I had at that time.
- ☐ I'd prefer something else, but I can deal with this too.
- ☐ I don't need someone's approval to be happy.

- ☐ This is painful, so I need to be extra kind and gentle to myself right now.
- ☐ You can't win them all.
- ☐ Things don't have to work out exactly as I expected for me to be happy.
- ☐ "Different" does not necessarily mean "better."
- ☐ I can sit through this and talk to my friend or mom or therapist to bitch later.
- ☐ Not everything will go my way, but I can work on being flexible.
- ☐ I'm allowed to experience my emotions fully and still be safe.
- ☐ There's no right way to do life; there are no real timelines.
- ☐ I am not responsible for fixing someone else's problems.
- ☐ I am not responsible for managing someone else's emotions.
- ☐ I am not responsible for someone else's behaviors.
- ☐ This feeling is uncomfortable, but it will pass through me slowly but surely.
- ☐ Just because I'm thinking something does not necessarily make it true.
- ☐ I'm having a human moment.
- ☐ Not my monkeys, not my circus.
- ☐ I can choose to restart my day at any point.
- ☐ I am allowed to make mistakes and then learn from them.
- ☐ You can't please everyone all the time.
- ☐ My emotions are transient; they come and go.
- ☐ I can pause and choose what to do next instead of acting impulsively.
- ☐ I give myself permission to not be perfect.
- ☐ For every tough moment I go through, I learn more and become more resilient.
- ☐ I've weathered tough days before, and I trust I can get through this one too.
- ☐ I don't have to solve everything right now. Small steps count.
- ☐ Advocating for myself is okay and doesn't make me mean or pushy.
- ☐ I'm willing to fail in order to find new ways to succeed later.
- ☐ Stop and breathe. I can do this.
- ☐ This will pass; nothing lasts forever.
- ☐ I have done this before, and I can do it again.
- ☐ I don't need to rush. I can take things slowly.
- ☐ I feel this way because of my past experiences, but I am safe right now.

☐ It's okay to feel this way. It's a normal reaction.

☐ Right now, I'm not in danger.

☐ Right now, I'm safe.

☐ I can use my coping skills and get through this.

☐ I am capable.

☐ I'm going to let this emotion move through my body and run its course.

☐ Do no harm, take no shit.

☐ This is an opportunity for me to learn how to cope with my fears.

☐ I can take all the time I need right now to relax and cope.

☐ I can learn from this, and next time will be easier.

☐ My body is allowed to change. That's part of being alive.

☐ I don't have to love my body to respect it and treat it kindly.

☐ How I feel about my body is not the truth of my body.

☐ Bodies are not meant to stay the same forever, or even day to day.

☐ I can choose not to punish myself for being human.

☐ This feeling is real, but it isn't a reliable narrator.

☐ How would I treat a young me in this moment?

☐ I'm allowed to wear the size that fits the body I have today.

☐ I don't need to shrink to be deserving of good things.

☐ My body is doing a hundred things for me right now that I'm not even noticing.

☐ I'm not going to war with myself over a pair of pants.

☐ The number on a tag or a scale doesn't measure my actual life in any real way.

☐ I don't owe anyone a certain body. Not even past versions of myself.

☐ This is a body-image thought, not a fact.

☐ I can let this wave come and go without attaching a story to it.

☐ This moment doesn't get to decide how I feel about myself long term.

☐ I'm allowed to take up space.

☐ I don't need to fix myself. I need to support myself.

☐ Other: ____________________

☐ Other: ____________________

☐ Other: ____________________

Make It Personal!

Think about a few distressing situations that come up for you often. Write down a specific coping thought you can use the next time you're in that situation.

1. Distressing situation:

 Coping thought:

2. Distressing situation:

 Coping thought:

3. Distressing situation:

 Coping thought:

Once you find a coping thought that actually lands for you, write it down somewhere you'll see it during the real moment. Put it in a Notes app, on your mirror, in your wallet, on a sticky note—wherever your brain is most likely to stumble into it when things feel rough. The goal is to make it easy to reach for when distress shows up, because nobody remembers their healthiest thoughts in the middle of a spiral. Having it visible gives you a lifeline you can grab without thinking!

Coping Ahead

Preparing for emotionally challenging situations ahead of time

At its core, coping ahead is about planning for a stressful situation before it happens, instead of being blindsided by it and scrambling in the moment. If distress tolerance is about getting through a painful moment without making it worse, coping ahead is about giving ourselves a head start.

This skill asks clients to prepare both internally and externally. Internally means identifying the thoughts, fears, urges, and emotions they tend to fall into when they're in distressing situations. Externally means picking the exact DBT skills that will serve them best and then mentally rehearsing how they'll apply them. Think of it as emotion regulation meets manifestation with a dash of sports psychology.

While clients often believe they'll "figure it out in the moment," the reality is that when emotions are overwhelming, the thinking brain goes offline. It has nothing to do with willpower or resilience—it's literal brain science. Having a plan makes the moment a bit less scary, while rehearsing the plan makes it a bit more familiar. And familiarity reduces reactivity. With this skill, clients are no longer walking into the situation empty-handed. They're walking in as badass cowboys (or gals!) armed with a pistol on their hip—a.k.a. a toolkit they've intentionally picked and practiced.

This is a great skill for clients who catastrophize, procrastinate, or dread future events. It gives them something active and empowering to do, increasing their sense of self-agency. Here are the steps to teach this skill.

Step 1: Imagine and Describe the Situation

Have the client walk you through a stressful situation that reliably comes up for them. This could be a big exam, a difficult conversation, a holiday meal with family, seeing an ex, or any other number of examples. Ask them to be as specific as possible. You want the details! What specifically tends to happen? What thoughts show up? What feelings get stirred? What urges spike? The more vivid their description, the easier it becomes to create a targeted plan.

Step 2: Choose the DBT Skills They Will Use

This is where coping ahead becomes personalized and effective. Instead of throwing every skill at the wall, help them pick the exact strategies that will work for that specific situation. Remember that in DBT, we do what's *effective*, meaning we don't choose the skills we "think" should work but in reality are a flop. We pick the skills that actually move the needle for us, whether or not it's the "perfect" skill. Who cares? Do what works!

Feel free to check out the full checklist of DBT skills on the accompanying client-facing worksheet so they can choose from a menu instead of having to remember all the DBT skills off the cuff. They might select:

- Opposite action for a triggering social event
- Check the facts for catastrophic thinking
- DEAR MAN for a boundary conversation
- TIPP for panic attacks
- Positive/neutral coping thoughts for performance anxiety
- Five senses grounding for rumination
- Radical acceptance for things outside their control

This part is the heart of the skill. Here, clients are not just predicting stress, they are predicting what they can do about it when it comes up.

Step 3: Rehearse the Plan in Their Mind

This is where our manifestation moment comes in, and honestly, it's one of my favorite parts. In DBT, we ask clients to mentally rehearse their coping plan with as much detail as possible. We encourage them to imagine:

- What they'll say
- What skills they'll use
- What sensations to expect
- How they want to respond
- What it will feel like to cope effectively

This visualization helps build behavioral muscle memory. It shifts the default expectation from "I'm going to fall apart" to "I know what I will do." It might sound silly and is very easy to skip, but don't! Trust the process because the brain needs rehearsal. Here's why it matters: When clients rehearse, they are training the nervous system to expect the stressful moment and to expect themselves to cope effectively in it. The brain does not fully distinguish between imagined and real experiences, so mental rehearsal strengthens the same neural pathways they use during the real situations. That's neuroplasticity in action!

This means when the moment actually happens, clients feel less startled, less overwhelmed, and more prepared. Their coping plan no longer feels theoretical. It feels familiar. And familiar is calming. Think of it like Neo dodging the slowed bullets in *The Matrix*: The bullets represent distress, and the dogging represents clients coping ahead and facing each moment as it comes—and, of course, looking like a badass while doing it.

If you want to take it up a notch, ask the client to rehearse multiple versions: the ideal scenario, the realistic scenario, and the "things go sideways" scenario. This prepares them across the board.

Session tip: Make the client actually walk through their rehearsal out loud. Have them get into a comfortable position, close their eyes, and walk you through the process in their mind's eye. You'll learn so much about their thinking.

Addressing Common Client Pitfalls

Although coping ahead can be an incredibly effective tool, some clients might expect perfection, try to do too much at once, or rehearse the stress rather than the coping itself. Here's how to overcome these common pitfalls:

- **Clients imagine themselves coping perfectly.**
  → Reinforce flexibility. The goal isn't perfection—it's effectiveness, even in small bits. Sometimes the coping plan will go exactly as rehearsed, and sometimes it'll go 60 percent right. And that still counts!
- **Clients pick too many skills at once.**
  → Help them narrow it down to the one or two skills that matter most. An overloaded plan becomes overwhelming and may cause them to end up using no skills as a result.
- **Clients only rehearse the stress, not the coping.**
  → Guide them back to the skill. They're not rehearsing the disaster; they are rehearsing the response. Encourage them to treat the rehearsal as if they're watching a scene of themselves being effective.
- **Clients treat the skill as a one-time activity.**
  → Normalize repetition. The more they rehearse, the stronger the neural pathway becomes!
- **Clients say, "I don't know what to do in the moment."**
  → Remind them: Coping ahead exists specifically for that reason—that's why we do this! Remember that this skill is a confidence builder. It trains clients to see themselves as capable before the moment even arrives. When they internalize that, everything shifts.

Client Worksheet

Coping Ahead

Preparing for emotionally challenging situations ahead of time

Coping ahead is a skill that helps you prepare for stressful situations *before* they happen so you can feel more confident and steady in the moment. This worksheet will walk you through imagining the stressful situation, choosing the coping skills you want to use, and rehearsing exactly how you'll handle it.

Step 1: Imagine and Describe the Situation

Describe a stressful or overwhelming situation you expect to face soon. Be specific. What usually happens in this situation? What thoughts or feelings tend to come up for you?

____

____

____

____

Step 2: What DBT Skills Do You Want to Use?

Think about the DBT skills you've learned. Which ones would genuinely help you cope effectively in this situation?

- ☐ WHAT and HOW skills
- ☐ Mindfulness of the Inner Critic
- ☐ Wise Mind
- ☐ Cognitive Distortions
- ☐ Nonjudgmental Stance
- ☐ Pocket Mindfulness
- ☐ Pocket Distress Tolerance (TIPP, ACCEPTS, STOP)
- ☐ Five Senses Grounding
- ☐ Making Lemonade from Lemons
- ☐ Coping Ahead
- ☐ Positive/Neutral Coping Thoughts
- ☐ Radical Acceptance
- ☐ Identifying Emotions
- ☐ PLEASE Skills
- ☐ Alternate Rebellion
- ☐ Opposite Action
- ☐ Checking the Facts
- ☐ Problem-Solving
- ☐ Behavioral Chain Analysis
- ☐ Building Mastery
- ☐ Assertiveness vs. Aggression
- ☐ DEAR MAN
- ☐ GIVE FAST
- ☐ Emotional Bank Account
- ☐ Understanding Boundaries
- ☐ Saying No with Confidence
- ☐ Receiving Feedback in Healthy Ways
- ☐ Blocks to Interpersonal Effectiveness
- ☐ Relapse Prevention Planning
- ☐ Dialectical Abstinence

Why did you choose these skills?

Step 3: Rehearse It in Your Mind

Imagine yourself in the situation using the coping skills you chose. Walk through it step by step. What will you think? What will you do? How will you move through the moment? Try to picture it as clearly as you can. Your brain responds to rehearsal just like real practice, so this coping skill will feel more natural and automatic when the moment arrives.

Step 4: If Things Don't Go as Planned

Sometimes the moment won't unfold exactly how you pictured it. What is a backup skill or coping plan you can use if things feel harder than expected?

Step 5: Final Check-In

Do you feel more prepared for this situation than before?

What part of your plan feels most supportive?

Radical Acceptance

Letting go of the fight that keeps suffering alive

Radical acceptance is one of the hardest DBT skills to teach and one of the most life-changing when it finally lands. I say this because it's true. The idea is simple but emotionally challenging. Radical acceptance asks us to accept reality as it is, fully with our mind, body, and spirit, without fighting against it or layering on judgments like "This shouldn't have happened" or "It's not fair." It's about acknowledging what *is*, even if we hate it, and choosing the most effective way forward.

The key here is that acceptance does *not* mean approval. It is not agreement, forgiveness, saying something is "fine," giving up, enabling bad behavior, letting people off the hook, or excusing injustice. It does not mean the situation is okay, justified, or morally acceptable. Some things in life are deeply unfair and devastating. Some things should never have happened. Radical acceptance is not about being at peace with injustice or saying it's okay that this thing happened. It's about recognizing that fighting reality keeps us stuck in suffering. In DBT, we have a quote that goes "Where we fight reality is where we invite in suffering." And what that refers to is the way our pain intensifies when we cling to how things "should" be instead of acknowledging how things actually are.

The more we resist, protest, replay, and grasp for a different version of the past, the more trapped we end up feeling. Acceptance doesn't erase the hurt, but it removes the extra layer of suffering that comes from arguing with a reality that isn't going to change. Radical acceptance is the moment we shift from "This shouldn't be happening" to "This is happening, and now what?" And that is where our power and freedom to act begins.

Radical acceptance is most helpful when clients are facing realities they unfortunately cannot change or undo. Some powerful examples include:

- Coping with a breakup or the end of a relationship
- Facing a chronic illness or ongoing physical pain
- Accepting the loss of a loved one or navigating grief
- Dealing with job loss, financial instability, or major life transitions
- Managing conflicts where the other person refuses to change
- Letting go of past mistakes or regrets
- Facing systemic, societal, or global hardships
- Accepting rejection or disappointment
- Accepting the limitations of others, such as a family member's persistent behavior

I like to introduce radical acceptance using the metaphor of a beach ball, which I have found clients never forget:

"Picture this: It's a gorgeous summer day and you're in the pool with friends, sipping lemonade, soaking up the sun, playing mermaids, and having a blast. Now, imagine there's a very ugly beach ball floating on the surface of the water. You hate this beach ball. It's messing up the vibe, getting in your way, and honestly, you just don't want to look at it. So you decide to hold it underwater to get it out of your sight.

But the harder you push it down, the harder it pushes back. Sometimes it even flies up and smacks you in the face. On top of that, keeping it submerged takes every ounce of your energy. You're no longer enjoying the sunshine or the cool water or the people around you. Your whole day becomes 'don't let this beach ball float up.'

This is exactly what happens when you fight reality. The more you try to push down reality, the stronger, louder, and more intrusive it becomes. Radical acceptance is like choosing to let that hideous little beach ball float in the pool with you. It doesn't mean you suddenly like the situation. It's still annoying, still unwanted, still ugly. But you stop wasting your energy on a fight you can't win. And the relief that follows is genuinely real. When you're no longer wrestling the beach ball, you finally have the capacity to engage with what's actually in front of you. You get the sunshine back. You get the water back. You get yourself back. That's the power of acceptance. It frees you from the ultimate exercise in futility."

Session tip: Use the beach ball metaphor often, especially with clients who suppress emotions. "Sounds like you're holding that beach ball underwater again!"

How to Teach This Skill

There are many ways to teach this skill, many of which unfortunately feel very conceptual and less practical. I'm going to give you the practical version!

- Start by asking the client to notice if they're fighting reality. Look for phrases like "should," "shouldn't," and "it's not fair," or any tightening in the body. Start by examining small, low-stakes situations before diving into trauma-level realities! Practice makes progress here.
- Review the facts of the situation as it is. No judgment. No backstory. Just reality as it currently exists.
- Acknowledge that this situation has causes—things don't just happen randomly. It's not about blaming anyone, but understanding that events unfold in a sequence or chain of events. Ask questions like "What led to this? What factors are at play here?" This helps the client shift from a place of shame to a place of clarity.

- Invite them to attend to body sensations. Are they feeling any tension, tightness, or heaviness? These physical sensations are all part of the acceptance process, even if they feel uncomfortable.
- Then encourage them to allow their emotions to arise. Acceptance often brings grief, sadness, disappointment, or even relief. Normalize that accepting and liking are two very different things.
- And for the *pièce de resistance,* explore the miracle question: "Let's imagine something for a moment. If you weren't radically accepting this situation, what would that look like? What would you be thinking, doing, saying, or obsessing over?"
    - Have your client list out all the behaviors, thoughts, impulses, and actions that show they are resisting the current reality. For example, if someone is struggling to accept a breakup, their "nonacceptance list" might include things like constantly checking their ex's social media, rereading old texts, replaying conversations, talking about the breakup with everyone they know, isolating, or trying to rehash things with the ex.
- Then shift the question: "Now imagine that somehow, some way, you woke up tomorrow and you had fully accepted this situation. You might still be sad, but you're no longer fighting reality. What would the *accepting* version of you be doing differently?"
    - Have your client create a second "acceptance" list regarding the situation. In the breakup example, that might look like deleting old text messages, archiving photos, muting or unfollowing their ex on social media, redirecting rumination when it starts, talking about other parts of life with loved ones, spending time with friends, or beginning to imagine future relationships.
- Once both lists are complete, ask the client to pick one or two behaviors from the acceptance list that feel doable right now, and practice doing them.

The best thing about this intervention is that it turns a very high-level conceptual skill into something practical and behavioral. By intentionally acting in ways that align with acceptance, the client begins sending their brain a new message: *I am moving forward*. In DBT language, this is essentially a form of opposite action—acting in ways that go against the natural urge to resist reality. When a client changes their behavior first, the emotional and cognitive shift toward acceptance often follows.

Addressing Common Client Pitfalls

As with any skill, radical acceptance can be challenging, but recognizing and addressing these common pitfalls can help clients stay on track:

- **Clients think acceptance means approval.**
  - → Correct them gently and often! Acceptance is about facing reality as it is, not endorsing it. It's the clinical equivalent of "It is what it is" or the native New Yorker version of "What are you gonna do?" with a very Tony Soprano shrug.
- **Clients expect to feel instant relief and think acceptance is a one-time thing.**
  - → Explain that acceptance is a practice. It gets easier with repetition. It's also an everyday process: Some days they will move closer toward acceptance, and some days they may find themselves further away. This is normal.
- **Clients jump straight into "fixing" instead of accepting.**
  - → Redirect them. You cannot fix what you refuse to acknowledge.
- **Clients think acceptance means no action.**
  - → Highlight that acceptance is the gateway to effective action, not the end point. Once they've accepted reality, they have the clarity to take action that matters rather than acting out of frustration.
- **Clients get stuck in self-blame.**
  - → Instead of spinning in circles about who's to blame, return the client to focusing on the causes of the situation ("What led to this?"), not who's at fault. Causes help us understand, blame keeps us stuck.

Use the accompanying client-facing worksheet to guide clients toward a clear picture of what acceptance would allow them to do next, and possibly even motivational interviewing questions that help them see the benefit of this, like "What would free up for you if we didn't spend so much time trying to change this?"

Client Worksheet

Radical Acceptance

Letting go of the fight that keeps suffering alive

Radical acceptance is a skill that helps you face reality as it is, not as you wish it were. It does not mean you approve of the situation. It means you stop fighting a reality you cannot change so that you can free up your energy to cope more effectively. Think of it like stopping the struggle with that ugly beach ball in the pool: When you stop pushing it underwater, you get your energy back—and you get to enjoy the sunshine again. Use this worksheet to help you move toward acceptance, one small step at a time.

Describe a current distressing situation in your life. Be as detailed and factual as you can.

____

____

____

What do you have control over in this situation?

____

____

____

What do you not have control over?

____

____

____

In what ways is fighting against reality hurting you (emotionally, physically, mentally, behaviorally)?

____

____

____

What does it look like when you do *not* accept this situation? What do you say, think, or do?

____

____

____

What is one small action you can take today that moves you toward the "accepting" version of yourself? (Think of doing the opposite action of what you listed in the previous step. Choose something doable and kind.)

What emotions come up when you think about accepting this situation?

What are some acceptance thoughts or phrases you can use when this situation comes up? (Examples: "This is what it is," "I don't have to like this to accept it," "I can stop fighting what I cannot change")

If you let the "beach ball" float instead of wrestling it underwater, what might it free up for you?

Crisis Survival Strategies When Distress Tolerance Isn't Enough

As you now know, distress tolerance skills are designed to help clients survive emotional pain without making the situation worse. They are all about getting through the moment safely when emotions feel intense, overwhelming, or uncomfortable. But part of doing DBT responsibly is being honest about this one hard truth: Not all distress is meant to be tolerated, and not all situations can be handled with skills alone! DBT is not about pushing through at all costs no matter what. It is about staying alive, staying safe, and knowing when to bring in more support if needed.

I wanted to include this section to help all the fabulous readers understand when distress tolerance skills are appropriate, when you need to shift into crisis survival mode, and when it is time to involve outside or higher-level support. Using this framework can help reduce shame for clients and hesitation for clinicians when things escalate.

When Distress Tolerance Is the Right Tool

Distress tolerance skills are most effective when a client is emotionally dysregulated but still able to pause, make choices, and engage in coping behaviors—think *within* their TLA. The client may feel miserable, panicky, angry, or overwhelmed, but they are not at severe acute risk of harming themselves or others. Their nervous system is activated, but they still have access to some level of control and decision-making.

Right here is the zone where skills like TIPP, STOP, ACCEPTS, self-soothing, grounding, and radical acceptance can do the heavy lifting. The goal here is not to feel better instantly but to get through the moment without impulsive or self-destructive behavior. As a clinician, you want to reinforce that using distress tolerance in these moments is all about strength, not avoidance. Clients are learning how to survive emotional waves without creating long-term consequences.

It can be helpful to normalize that distress tolerance often feels unsatisfying, and honestly a bit boring and anticlimactic. Clients may say, "This doesn't fix anything," and they are sort of right! Distress tolerance is not a fix, but also, it's not meant to be. (That's why it's called distress tolerance, not distress elimination!) At its core, distress tolerance is meant to be the bridge that gets them from an intense emotion to a place where problem-solving, emotion regulation, or interpersonal skills can happen later.

When Distress Becomes a Crisis

In DBT, a crisis is not defined by how uncomfortable someone feels—it's defined by safety. Distress crosses into crisis territory when a client feels unable to keep themselves safe, when urges feel highly uncontrollable, or when the risk of harm is rising quickly. This might include active suicidal ideation, strong urges to self-harm, dangerous substance use, severe dissociation, or a sense of being completely overwhelmed and out of control.

In these moments, asking a client to "just use their skills" can feel invalidating on a good day, and dangerous on a bad one. Enter: crisis survival strategies. This is where the primary goal shifts from emotional coping to immediate safety protocols. The focus becomes staying alive, reducing risk, and accessing support.

I often explain this to clients using a physical health comparison. If you are sore after a workout, you stretch, rest, and heat/ice. If your leg is broken, you go to the hospital. Emotional pain works the same way. Some pain can be worked through with skills, while other pain requires immediate attention and support. Knowing the difference is a sign of wisdom, both for us and our clients.

As a clinician, you want to work with your clients to help them be efficient at identifying their personal warning signs that indicate they are moving from distress into crisis. These warning signs are often deeply individual, but they tend to fall into a few key categories. Some clients notice changes in their thoughts. This might sound like "I can't do this anymore," "Nothing will help," or "I just need the pain to stop." Others notice it in their body, such as intense agitation (e.g., rocking, nonstop movement), numbness, a buzzing or vibrating feeling, chest tightness, or a sense of being outside their body. For some clients, the shift shows up in behavior, like pacing, isolating, impulsively reaching for substances, giving away belongings, or feeling an urgent need to escape. And for many, the clearest red flag is a surge in urges that feel louder, faster, and harder to resist than usual. By learning to name these warning signs, it will become much easier and effective to move into crisis survival mode.

When Distress Tolerance Isn't Enough and Outside Support Is Needed

There are times when DBT skills, even when used beautifully, are not sufficient on their own ☹. This is not a flaw in DBT, the client, or us for that matter. DBT was designed to work alongside crisis resources, emergency services, and higher levels of care when needed.

You have permission to escalate care without guilt or hesitation. Encouraging a client to call a crisis line, contact a trusted support person, go to the emergency room, or engage in a higher level of care is not "giving up." It is practicing effective, ethical treatment. I know it can sometimes be a bit of a hit to the ego because we want to be the ones to help. And it's fair and human that we want that. At the same time, knowing when something is out of our scope *is* us doing our job and making sure the client gets to safety. If you were a podiatrist, you wouldn't treat someone with cardiac arrest, right? You'd send them to an acute cardiovascular surgeon. Maybe Christina Yang from *Grey's Anatomy*. You get the point. It's okay if you can't help with everything your clients might be dealing with.

How you frame outside support to your clients matters a lot because this can be a delicate matter to discuss. You should present it as a tool, not a punishment. It's always useful to remind clients that their need for extra help does not mean they are "too much" or "doing DBT wrong." It simply means the intensity of the moment exceeds what skills alone can manage, and part of your job is to help clients see asking for help as an act of self-respect and survival. Here are some tips for crisis survival planning.

Plan Ahead

Crisis survival planning should *always* happen when clients are not in crisis. All these tools and protocols are best ironed out when clients are in Wise Mind and able to make clear and healthy decisions. In my experience, planning ahead increases the likelihood that clients will actually use supports when they need them.

I recommend proactively walking through the extremely practical details of a crisis plan even when it feels unnecessary. This is your and your client's emergency brake if needed. This includes identifying nearby hospitals or emergency rooms that look safe and accessible, which ones accept the client's insurance, and what going there would realistically look like. What you are trying to do here is reduce uncertainty ahead of time because when clients are already in crisis, entering into a new and unknown plan can be extremely scary. It's also important to identify who they might contact for support, who could go with them if needed, and which environments feel safest or most grounding for them.

Go for Meds

For some clients, medication can be part of a crisis survival plan. PRN medications (meaning they're taken as needed instead of every day), such as clonazepam or propranolol, when prescribed appropriately, can help reduce physiological overwhelm enough for clients to access skills and support. This is all about stabilizing the nervous system and getting to a place where the skills can actually land.

For clients who live in a near-constant state of crisis or survival mode, psychopharmacology can be incredibly helpful. A low-dose SSRI or mood stabilizer can help lower baseline emotional intensity so DBT skills become more usable and sustainable. I know some people may not be open to this option, and if they aren't, that's okay. If they are, remind them that medication is not a failure of therapy; rather, it is a support that allows therapy to work more effectively. If they struggled with diabetes, they would take insulin right? This is no different just because it's mental and not physical. Medicine is medicine.

MODULE 3

Emotion Regulation

Emotion Regulation: The Quick and Dirty

If I had to sum up emotion regulation in one sentence, it would be this: Emotion regulation is about increasing pleasant emotions and decreasing unnecessary suffering.

Notice I did not say "getting rid of emotions," because that's not the goal here. Emotions are not the enemy. In fact, they can be rich data. Emotion regulation skills exist simply to keep our emotional system healthy and functioning—not muted, not shut down, and not constantly running the show and dictating our behaviors.

At its core, emotion regulation skills teach us a few key things: how to accurately identify what we are feeling, how intense those feelings are, and what emotional patterns tend to show up for us over time. It helps us understand why emotions show up in the first place, how they're trying to help, and how we can respond in ways that make things better, not worse. With emotion regulation skills, we start to experience our emotions as signals and sources of information, instead of emergencies.

One of my favorite quotes from DBT is "Everyone struggles, but only some people suffer." That line can feel a little provocative at first, especially for clients who already feel overwhelmed or invalidated, so let me break it down a bit.

DBT is not saying that some people have easy lives and others do not. Quite the contrary! Everyone experiences pain, loss, disappointment, rejection, and stress—all that jazz. The difference is not the presence of struggle. It's how someone experiences—and in turn *responds* to—that struggle. Suffering tends to happen when emotions feel confusing, overwhelming, or unmanageable, as well as when people do not have the skills, access, or willingness to respond to those emotions effectively.

Two people can go through the same difficult event and have very different internal experiences. One person may feel intense emotions but have tools to ride it out, while the other may feel just as much emotion but get stuck in panic, shame, self-blame, or impulsive reactions that make things worse. Emotion regulation skills are the bridge to that gap. These skills don't prevent pain, but they can dramatically reduce how much that pain turns into long-term suffering.

When I explain this skill to my clients, I often use the parable of the farmer and the mule, which sticks with them far longer than any acronym ever could:

> *"Once upon a time, there was a farmer who owned an old mule. One day, the mule fell into the farmer's well. The farmer heard the mule braying, or whatever mules do when they fall into wells.*

After carefully assessing the situation, the farmer sympathized with the mule but ultimately decided that neither the mule nor the well was worth the trouble of saving. Instead, he called his neighbors together, told them what happened, and enlisted them to help haul dirt to bury the old mule in the well and put him out of his misery.

Initially, the old mule was hysterical! But as the farmer and his neighbors continued shoveling, and the dirt hit his back, a thought struck the old mule. It suddenly dawned on him that every time a shovel load of dirt landed on his back, he could shake it off and step up onto that dirt!

So this he did, blow after blow, while repeating to himself, 'Shake it off and step up . . . Shake it off and step up . . . Shake it off and step up!' to encourage himself. No matter how painful the blows became or distressing the situation seemed, the old mule fought his panic and kept right on shaking it off and stepping up.

It wasn't long before the old mule, battered and exhausted, stepped triumphantly over the wall of that well. What seemed like would bury him actually blessed him, all because of the manner in which he handed his adversity.

That's life! If we face our problems and respond to them positively—refusing to give in to panic, bitterness, or self-pity—the adversities that come along to bury us usually have within them the potential to benefit and bless us."

That story is emotion regulation in a nutshell if you ask me. Life is going to throw dirt at us—stress, loss, triggers, disappointment, rejection, all that good stuff. Unfortunately, we do not get a vote on that part. But what we *do* get a vote on is what we do when the dirt hits us. Do we panic and freeze? Do we collapse into self-pity or bitterness? Or do we learn how to shake it off, step up, and respond in a way that moves us forward?

Massive disclaimer for this module: Emotion regulation skills are not about pretending things are fine. They're about learning how to work *with* emotions instead of against them. When clients successfully learn these skills, they stop feeling like their emotions are something happening *to* them and start feeling like they have some agency in how they respond.

Identifying Emotions

How emotions work and how to recognize them

Before clients can regulate their emotions, change their behaviors, or choose effective coping strategies, they need to know what they are *actually* feeling. Most folks come in using the "big four" emotional categories: happy, sad, angry, and anxious. While those labels are not necessarily wrong in some moments, they are often too broad to be helpful.

The goal of this skill is emotional clarity and specificity. When clients can name their emotions more specifically, they are *much* better able to respond to them effectively. For example, "frustrated" requires a different approach than "enraged," just as "lonely" calls for something different than "ashamed." Precision really does matter here, so let me bore you with an analogy that I like to use with clients:

> *"Imagine you're not feeling great, so you go to the doctor's office and they ask what brings you in today. If you say, 'I don't know, I just don't feel well,' the doctor might take a guess, but chances are the treatment they recommend won't fully address what's really going on. Now, if you describe exactly what you're feeling—'I have a sharp pain in my stomach; it gets worse after I eat, and I've been feeling nauseous and fatigued for two days'—the doctor can better narrow down the problem and provide a much more targeted treatment.*
>
> *It might seem silly, but emotions work in the same way. When you use broad, catchall labels like* bad or upset*, it's like telling the doctor, 'I don't feel well.' But when you can slow it down a bit and identify specific emotions—like rejection, disappointment, or overwhelm—it's like giving the doctor the detailed symptoms. The more specific you get with naming your emotions, the better equipped you are to understand what's truly going on and choose the most effective DBT skill to respond to it. In DBT, we call this 'Name it to tame it!'"*

For some clients, naming their emotions might come naturally, but many people were never taught how to identify emotions beyond basic labels. Some may have even learned to suppress their emotions, push them away, intellectualize them, or jump straight into problem-solving. I like to remind people that struggling to identify emotions is not a personal flaw, it's more of a skill gap, honestly. And the good news is, they have the ability to learn these skills, even if it is later in life!

What Are Emotions?

When providing clients with psychoeducation about emotions, I like to start by explaining what emotions are: biological signals. At their core, emotions are chemical and electrical responses that provide information, prepare the body for action, and influence behavior. This explanation can reduce shame around certain emotions and remind clients that emotions are quite functional, even when they're uncomfortable. Here is a quick breakdown of why each emotion exists:

- **Happiness** signals that something is good, beneficial, or aligned with our values, encouraging us to seek more of it and reinforcing behaviors that promote well-being.

- **Sadness** helps us process loss, signals a need for support, and slows us down to reflect, allowing us to adjust and heal from difficult experiences.
- **Anxiety** heightens awareness of potential threats, preparing us to take action, plan ahead, or avoid danger, even when the threat isn't immediate.
- **Shame** serves as a social regulator, signaling when we've violated personal or societal values and prompting us to repair relationships or realign with our morals.
- **Anger** energizes us to respond to perceived injustice, set boundaries, and protect ourselves or others when something feels unfair or threatening.
- **Fear** activates our survival instincts, preparing us to escape or defend against danger and helping us stay safe in potentially harmful situations.
- **Guilt** nudges us to recognize when we've harmed someone or acted against our values, motivating us to make amends and grow from our mistakes.
- **Disgust** protects us from physical or moral contamination, helping us avoid harmful substances, behaviors, or situations that could be dangerous.
- **Love** strengthens social bonds, fostering connection, care, and cooperation, which are essential for survival and emotional well-being.
- **Jealousy** signals a fear of loss, often in relationships, prompting us to protect or strengthen our connections and clarify what we value.

After normalizing the functions of emotions, I like to play a little game with my clients. It might sound stupid, but hear me out. I bring up a blank Word document on my computer and ask them to name as many emotions as they possibly can. I encourage them to name everything that comes to mind, even if emotions feel similar or overlapping. What I have found over the years of doing this is that most clients run out of words quickly (about ten minutes in)—and that moment of "I'm stuck; there are no more emotions" is the point. It highlights how limited emotional language can keep people stuck in a space of vague distress.

Once clients hit that wall, I show them an extended emotions list. I like using the one from Tom Drummond, but feel free to use whatever works for you. As we review the expanded list together, they discover several emotions they hadn't thought of. It demonstrates that some emotions can be so subtle—and so tricky to name—that upping their emotional literacy is a worthwhile skill. The overall takeaway is that the more precisely we can name our emotions, the more we can choose effective coping strategies, which leads to less discomfort in the long run.

Emotions vs. Body States

It is common for people to confuse emotions with physical states or to use the word *feeling* to describe things that are actually body conditions. So to clarify: Emotions are biologically driven response systems like anger, fear, sadness, shame, or joy. They show up with thoughts, urges, and physical sensations all at once. Feelings, on the other hand, are the conscious experience and language we use to describe those emotions. For example, the emotion "fear" might come with a racing heart and an urge to escape, and the feeling might be "I feel scared" or "I feel anxious."

On the other hand, physical states like tired, hungry, sick, or overstimulated are not really emotions. They are, however, physical conditions that can significantly increase emotional vulnerability, so it makes sense why these get lumped together sometimes! When clients say, "I feel tired," it's helpful to validate their lived experience while also helping them look underneath the fatigue. Maybe the tiredness is making them more irritable, so anger shows up faster. Maybe it's amplifying sadness, leading to tearfulness or withdrawal. Or maybe it's feeding overwhelm, where even small tasks feel impossible. Naming the emotion underneath the fatigue helps clients respond more skillfully instead of just pushing through or judging themselves for feeling "off."

And always remember: If clients minimize this skill or see it as "too basic," remind them that emotion regulation starts with awareness. You can't regulate what you can't name, right?

The Transient Nature of Emotions

For many people (therapists included!), one of the hardest parts about intense emotions is not just how uncomfortable they feel in the moment, but how convincing they can be. When an emotion is strong enough, it feels . . . endless. Like the feeling will never shift, soften, or let up. This is especially true for emotions like anxiety, shame, sadness, or anger. When they take over, our brains tell us a very convincing story that this state is permanent.

This is where DBT gently reminds us of something important: Emotions are temporary. Say it with me, TEMPORARY. Even the most intense ones rise, peak, and fall. They do not stay forever, even when it feels like they will. Emotions operate more like waves than fixed states. They come in, move through, and eventually pass. However, when we are in the middle of a strong emotional wave, it can feel impossible to believe. That's when a visual or a story can help, especially when logic isn't enough. Here is one that I personally use.

When I am feeling overwhelmed by an emotion, I picture myself sitting on my couch. In my mind, the emotion is personified as someone else in the room with me. (Sometimes I even picture characters from *Big Mouth*, like the Depression Kitty or Tito the Anxiety Mosquito.) The more intense the emotion feels, the closer it is to me. When my anxiety is really loud, she is practically sitting on my lap. I cannot ignore her. She feels all consuming.

As time moves forward, even if I am not doing anything special to make the emotion go away, I notice a little shift. The emotion *slowly* gets off my lap and stands in front of me. She's still there—I can feel her—but she is not as overwhelming as before. As more time passes, she drifts toward the door. Step by step, she moves farther away, until eventually, she leaves the room and closes the door behind her. "Don't let the door hit you on the way out!" I think in my mind.

That does not mean she is gone forever, though. Just like any visitor, she might come back from time to time. But the point is that she does not stay permanently, and more importantly, she does not define the room.

This example is perhaps a little silly, but it helps me remember that emotions are experiences, not identities. Feeling anxious does not mean I *am* anxiety. Feeling sad does not mean I will *always* feel sad. Feeling overwhelmed does not mean I *am* broken. It means an emotion is visiting. And just like visitors, it will stay a while and eventually leave.

What's important to remember here is that DBT does not ask us to get rid of emotions or pretend they are not there. It asks us to notice them, name them, and ride them without acting in ways that make things worse. When we remember that our emotions are transient, it really can be a massive game changer for so many because then we can focus less on escaping them and more on allowing them to move through us. Think of it like metabolizing a meal: It's working its way through the body.

Sometimes the most effective thing clients can do with an emotion is let it sit with them on the couch for a while, trusting that eventually, it will stand up and walk itself out.

Client Worksheet

Identifying Emotions

How emotions work and how to recognize them

Before you can change how you respond to emotions, you need to know what you are actually feeling. Many of us rely on a few big emotional "catchall" words like happy, sad, angry, or anxious. These words are not necessarily wrong, but they are often too broad to help you understand what is really happening on a deeper level so that you can respond to them more effectively.

This worksheet is about building that emotional clarity. Remember that the beginning of emotion regulation is all about awareness, never judgment. Your goal is simply to start noticing your emotional patterns so you can respond with more intention, clarity, and self-compassion over time.

Let's break it down into steps.

Step 1: Understanding Emotions

What exactly are emotions? Emotions are biological signals—automatic responses in your body and brain that give you information, prepare you for action, and influence behavior. It's important to remember that emotions are neither good nor bad. They just kind of . . . *are*. There's no doubt that some emotions are more pleasant to sit through than others, but even the most uncomfortable emotions are functional, and a lot of the time, they're trying to tell you something.

Different emotions serve different purposes. For example, sadness can signal a loss and a need for support. Anxiety can help you prepare for potential danger. Anger can alert you to unfairness or boundaries that might have been crossed. Shame can signal that something isn't aligned with your values. When you understand what an emotion is doing, you can respond more skillfully instead of reacting on autopilot!

Step 2: Emotions vs. Body States

Sometimes when people say "I feel . . ." they're actually describing a physical state, not an emotion. Being tired, hungry, sick, or overstimulated are not emotions. They are body conditions that can make emotions stronger and harder to manage, and they can leave us feeling more vulnerable. For example, when you say, "I feel tired," that might be true, but there might also be emotion underneath or intensified by that tiredness. Being exhausted can make anger flare faster, sadness feel heavier, and overwhelm take over more easily. Both your body state and your emotions matter when doing this work!

Step 3: Emotion Brain Dump

Because so many of us were never taught the language for emotions beyond a few basic words, it's hard later in life to accurately identify them for ourselves. Let's have a little fun with it for a second—this part is meant to be educational, not a graded exam! So without overthinking it, write down as many emotions as you can think of. Similar or overlapping emotions are allowed. There are no wrong answers!

Pause for a moment and notice what this exercise was like for you:

☐ Easy ☐ Hard ☐ I got stuck quickly!

Step 4: Expanding Your Emotional Vocabulary

Now take a look at an expanded list of emotions (like the one on page 224 of this book). As you read through it, notice what comes up for you. Many people are surprised by how many emotion words they didn't think of on their own. That's totally normal and okay! As you review the list, reflect on the following questions.

How many emotion words on the list did you not write down earlier but recognize as ones you experience often?

Were there any emotion words that made you think, "Oh yeah, that one hits"? Which ones?

Step 5: Noticing Your Emotional Patterns

Now zoom out a bit and think about your emotional world more broadly. Which emotions do you notice yourself experiencing most often?

Which emotions do you experience less often or tend to avoid or push away?

Are there any emotions that you suspect might be present underneath the surface, even if they don't always get named out loud? These might be emotions that show up as irritability, shutdown, numbness, overthinking, or feeling "off" without knowing why.

What emotions do you think you'd want to pay a little more attention to moving forward?

Step 6: The Transient Nature of Emotions

One important thing to remember about emotions is that they are temporary experiences, not permanent states. Even when an emotion feels overwhelming, it usually rises, peaks, and eventually passes if you allow it to move through you rather than fight against it.

Take a moment to reflect on how emotions tend to show up for you. Which emotions tend to linger longer when they appear in your life?

Which emotions tend to pass more quickly once they show up?

Are there any emotions that seem to come in strong waves but fade with time, especially if you give them space? Which ones?

What have you noticed helps certain emotions soften or move through you more easily?

PLEASE Skills

Understanding how your physical state impacts your emotions more than you might think

Buckle up, another acronym! PLEASE stands for: treat PhysicaL illness, practice balanced Eating, avoid mood-Altering substances, get balanced Sleep, and Exercise. These skills live in the emotion regulation module for a reason. Before you ask clients to manage intense emotions, tolerate distress, or change their behaviors, it's always a good idea to look at the physical foundation those emotions are sitting on. Why? Because sometimes the most effective ways to regulate emotions are the simplest.

Many clients come into therapy frustrated with themselves for being "too emotional" or "overreacting." Enter PLEASE skills, which target the physical vulnerabilities that make emotions faster, stronger, and harder to regulate—like a tiny gremlin running around behind the scenes, flipping emotional switches without permission. PLEASE skills help reframe this experience by shifting the question from "What's wrong with me?" to "What's happening in my body right now?"

This skill is essentially DBT's expanded version of HALT (Hungry, Angry, Lonely, Tired), which is used in Alcoholics Anonymous (AA) and Narcotics Anonymous (NA). The core idea is simple but powerful: When the body is depleted, stressed, underfed, tired, or sick, emotions have less room to move through the system without tipping into dysregulation. Clients are not "failing" at emotion regulation when they are exhausted, hungry, sick, or overwhelmed. They are just operating on an empty tank. I always think of those "You're not yourself when you're hungry" Snickers commercials when I talk about this, particularly the Betty White one.

That's why when it comes to emotion regulation, we start with PLEASE skills. You may not need to do a lengthy deep dive into opposite action or a full behavioral chain analysis if what a client really needs is a nutrient dense meal, a good night's sleep, and a little movement to get themselves right. Start simple first. If more skills are needed, then move to more.

When introducing the five main areas of PLEASE, you don't have to teach them as lectures or nutritional lessons. However, I do like to review why each one matters, as I find that clients respond well to the science behind it, so they know I'm not just giving them "woo-woo" self-care advice but strategies that actually support emotion regulation. That understanding increases buy-in, which is especially helpful for skeptical clients:

- **PL:** Being sick, in pain, or physically run down can increase emotional sensitivity, which is why it's so important to tend to illness and stress with care and compassion.
- **E:** Eating in a balanced, consistent way supports stable blood sugar and brain function, whereas restriction and overeating can send emotions on a roller coaster (with a side of shame).

- **A:** Mood-altering substances like drugs and alcohol interfere with emotional processing, impulse control, and nervous system regulation, making emotions harder to manage.
- **S:** A tired brain is a cranky brain. Getting enough sleep allows the brain to repair itself, regulate neurotransmitters, and process emotions effectively.
- **E:** Getting regular exercise helps stabilize mood, lower stress, and balance the nervous system.

To be clear: The goal of PLEASE skills is not perfection or rigid lifestyle rules. It's about stacking the deck in clients' favor by reducing unnecessary emotional vulnerability wherever possible.

How to Use the Worksheet in Session

The accompanying client-facing worksheet works best when framed as a curious check-in of sorts rather than a behavior audit. It's helpful to start by giving a simple explanation about how our physical states can greatly affect our emotional states. Feel free to throw in some examples so they can connect to this idea ("Have you ever gotten hangry? Or experienced 'hangxiety' after a night of drinking?"). Then, invite clients to notice how their particular patterns in eating, sleep, movement, substance use, and physical health might be affecting their emotional experiences—for better and for worse. If they become overwhelmed by the worksheet (which is completely normal because it's *a lot* of information) try to help them focus on one or two areas rather than all of them at once.

This is also a good moment to collaboratively (and nonjudgmentally!) explore the temporary rewards versus long-term costs of their behaviors. Bonus points for mentioning that this naturally invites dialectics into the conversation because it opens up space to discuss how something can help in the short term *and* hurt in the long term. For example, a client might describe how drinking lowers their anxiety in the moment, which we know is because alcohol increases GABA (gamma-aminobutyric acid) activity, the brain's primary calming neurotransmitter. At the same time, we can gently hold another truth: Over time, repeated alcohol use leads the brain to adapt by becoming less responsive to GABA while ramping up excitatory stress systems. That means when the alcohol wears off, the nervous system is left more activated than before—ultimately worsening baseline anxiety.

In my experience, it's quite common for folks to minimize this skill or see it as "basic" or "common sense," which, in all fairness, makes sense because to the naked eye, it's like telling someone who is extremely emotionally dysregulated to "just get a good night's sleep." It's your job to remind clients that although something may be common sense, that does not make it common *practice*, especially under stress. It's okay to normalize the annoying parts of this skill while also highlighting its utility!

Some clients may also feel some shame around their eating habits, substance use, or sleep struggles. These topics can be delicate, so you want to do your best to emphasize that PLEASE skills are about support, not control, and most certainly not about judgment. Other clients may feel discouraged by chronic illness, pain, or life stressors that they can't easily change, and this frustration is completely valid. While changing patterns might be simple and straightforward for some, for others it may feel impossible given their medical history or life circumstances. Here's where I like to reinforce that the goal is not to eliminate all PLEASE concerns, but to manage them more skillfully and compassionately, making microchanges when possible.

Big disclaimer: The PLEASE skills do not—I repeat, do not—eliminate uncomfortable emotions. They work to reduce any unnecessary emotional vulnerability clients might be carrying. When the body is cared for, emotions become more tolerable, clearer, and easier to respond to skillfully. That's all! It's a good reminder for clients who might have expectations that these skills will cure them. If only, right?

Client Worksheet

PLEASE Skills

Understanding how your physical state impacts your emotions more than you might think

Emotions do not exist in a vacuum. They live in the body, and when the body is stressed, depleted, sick, underfed, overtired, or overwhelmed, emotions tend to feel more intense, harder to manage—and on top of all that, quicker to spiral. But DBT has a solution for that! They are called PLEASE skills, and they focus on taking care of the physical foundations that support your ability to regulate your emotions. This isn't about being perfect or changing all your behaviors at once. It's about noticing where some small changes, or even microshifts, in how you care for your body might make your emotions easier to live with. Let's go over each PLEASE skill with a bit of an explanation.

PhysicaL Health and Illness

When your body is dealing with illness, chronic pain, inflammation, or ongoing physical stress, the nervous system is working overtime. This increases your emotional sensitivity and drastically lowers your tolerance for frustration. Even minor illnesses like a cold or a small injury can make your emotions feel way bigger and harder to manage. Supporting your physical health whenever possible is one of the more straightforward things you can do to reduce this background noise so your emotional system does not have to do as much heavy lifting.

Reflection: How does your physical health seem to impact your mood or emotional reactions? How do you feel emotionally when you are sick? Are there ways you might support your body more when you are sick, in pain, or run down?

___

___

Eating Patterns and Nutrition

The brain needs steady fuel to regulate emotions effectively. Think of it like a car needing gas. You wouldn't expect your car to run well on fumes, and your brain isn't any different. Irregular eating, restriction, bingeing and purging, or frequent blood sugar dips can drastically increase irritability, anxiety, emotional reactivity, and difficulty concentrating. Eating in a more balanced and consistent way helps stabilize blood sugar and supports the brain chemicals involved in mood regulation. It is about giving your brain the literal fuel that it needs to function.

Reflection: How do your current eating patterns seem to affect your mood, energy, or emotional reactivity? Are there small changes that might help you feel more stable throughout the day? Do you ever get hangry or feel overwhelmed when overly full?

Mood-Altering Substances

This is a no-brainer, but it's sometimes forgotten about. Substances like alcohol and drugs can temporarily change how you feel by altering your brain chemistry in a very real, concrete way. For example, alcohol increases calming neurotransmitters like GABA in the short term, which can make anxiety feel lower in the moment (hence feeling more relaxed or happy when you are drinking). But over time, repeated use can lead the brain to pull an UNO reverse—it becomes less effective at calming itself naturally, increasing baseline anxiety and emotional reactivity once the substance wears off. This can create a cycle where relief is short term but the emotional distress increases long term. How fun! And that is just alcohol. Other substances have their own way of altering brain chemistry that might feel okay—or even great—in the moment, but in the days (or sometimes even weeks) after, can make it harder to regulate emotionally.

Reflection: What substances do you use that you notice might impact your ability to successfully regulate your emotions (whether it be at the time of intoxication or in the days following)?

Sleep

Do not sleep on your sleep! Sleep is one of the most powerful regulators of emotional health, but it so often flies under the radar. During sleep, the brain restores neurotransmitter balance, processes emotions, and resets your stress response. When sleep is limited or inconsistent, your emotions often become more intense, less flexible, and harder to recover from. Think about a time you were so tired you found yourself crying over a TV commercial or the wrong coffee order. Poor sleep is not a personal flaw and does not mean you are failing at emotional regulation. It just means your system is depleted and could use a little restoring.

Reflection: How do your sleep patterns affect your emotions the next day? What patterns do you notice when you are well-rested versus overtired?

Exercise and Movement

Movement supports emotional regulation by releasing mood-boosting neurotransmitters, lowering stress hormones like cortisol, and helping the nervous system shake off built-up tension. Disclaimer: This does not have to mean you have to do an intense workout every day. Even gentle, consistent movement can do wonders for your mood, emotional resilience, and stress tolerance. No need for a daily ten-mile run (unless that's your jam).

Reflection: How have you noticed that movement, or lack of movement, affects your mood? What kinds of movement feel realistic and supportive for you to do in the spirit of emotional regulation?

____

____

Honorable Mentions: Life Stuff That Totally Counts Too

Before we wrap this up, it's important to name a few factors that can absolutely throw off emotional regulation, even though they don't fit neatly into the acronym. Big life transitions like traveling, moving, starting a new job, ending a relationship, getting married, having a baby, or even planning something exciting can seriously tax the nervous system! Stress is stress to the body, even when it's "good" stress. Your system still has to adjust, adapt, and recalibrate, which often means emotions feel bigger, more reactive, or harder to regulate for a while. That doesn't mean you're doing anything wrong. It means you're human and your nervous system is responding to change.

Shout-out to hormones too! Experiences like pregnancy, postpartum changes, fertility treatments, and monthly hormonal shifts related to menstruation can significantly impact mood, energy, emotional sensitivity, and stress tolerance. These changes are biological, and not a lack of coping skills or willpower. If you notice that emotional regulation is more difficult during certain life periods or stages, that information is power. It allows you to not only ride the wave more successfully, but also to reduce shame and lean into your PLEASE skills to make the ride a little less bumpy.

Reflection: Are there any current life changes, stressors, or hormonal factors that might be affecting your emotional regulation right now? How might you adjust your expectations, supports, or self-care during these periods?

____

____

Putting It All Together

Remember that these PLEASE skills are about reducing unnecessary emotional vulnerability, not eliminating emotions or forcing change. Improving even one physical area can make emotions feel more manageable without directly targeting the emotion itself. Small shifts count!

Reflection: Looking at these areas, which ones do you feel are the most important to focus on? Which ones feel like they need less attention at the moment? What is one small, realistic change you would like to experiment with?

Alternate Rebellion

How to rebel without burning your whole life down

Alternate rebellion is one of DBT's most underrated emotion regulation skills, especially for clients who have a strong oppositional streak, a history of self-destructive behaviors, a deep resistance to being told what to do, or just a general need to rebel. If you ever have a client who seems noncompliant with treatment, it's likely not because they don't care. Noncompliance often happens when autonomy matters deeply to someone! This skill honors that truth rather than fighting it.

At its core, alternate rebellion allows us to make space for defiance, individuality, intensity, or risk-taking urges in ways that are nondestructive and still aligned with a client's long-term goals. Why? Because suppressing rebellious urges can lead them to explode into self-harm, substance use, disordered eating, or impulsive behavior if that itch isn't scratched. With alternate rebellion, we aim to help clients redirect that energy into safer outlets—not to eliminate the need to rebel, but to channel it.

I have found that this skill is particularly effective for clients who struggle in a few specific areas: substance use, disordered eating, self-harm, chronic boredom, identity struggles, or a history of authority conflict. It also works beautifully with teens, young adults, and anyone who secretly identifies as a rule-breaker at heart. To be so honest, I use this *all the time*!

When teaching this skill, I think the name of the game is to lean into validation and humor by saying something like "Some people are natural-born rule-followers. Some people are natural-born rebels. DBT is not in the business of turning rebels into rule-followers. We just want to keep you alive and out of jail and safe." Framing it this way helps clients feel seen instead of corrected.

I like to explain that rebellion itself is not the problem. It's the form that the rebellion takes. We can break rebellion up into two categories: destructive rebellion and alternative rebellion. Destructive rebellion comes with consequences. Alternate rebellion lets clients still act out, push back, or feel edgy without sabotaging their goals or having the negative consequences.

Important disclaimer: Let's emphasize safety and values here. Although alternate rebellion is meant to allow clients to act out, it should not cause harm to self or others, create legal trouble, or undermine treatment goals. Within those boundaries, creativity is encouraged, and clients can really find something that allows them to say, "F you, world," but in a controlled, nonconsequential way.

Coaching the Skill

After introducing the skill, you want to help clients identify the situations where rebellious urges show up most strongly for them. They might mention times when they feel controlled, bored, invalidated, pressured, or emotionally numb. I would even go as far as asking them what the specific consequences are that they experience from their own brand of destructive rebellion.

Once those bits are clearly identified, you want to work collaboratively to build a personalized menu of alternate rebellion behaviors they can turn to instead.

Some clients might find some of the alternate rebellion skills to be a bit cheesy, but I really like to encourage them to choose the options that genuinely feel rebellious to them, not what they think they "should" choose. And what feels rebellious is highly personal! For one client, it might be loud music and bold clothes. For another, it might be saying no, being honest, or doing something spontaneous and out of character. Remind clients that the point is not productivity or self-improvement. The point is expression. If it feels a little silly, dramatic, or indulgent, they're probably on the right track.

Addressing Common Client Pitfalls

Some clients may feel skeptical, defensive, or uncertain about alternate rebellion when you first introduce it to them. Here's how those reactions typically show up and how to respond:

- **Clients think the skill sounds immature or irresponsible, like they're being encouraged to act out.**
  - → What this skill is actually doing is teaching clients to be smart about their patterns. The client already knows they have a rebellious side. Ignoring it or shaming it just makes it come out sideways. This skill is about giving that part of them a safer outlet so it doesn't take over in ways that hurt them. That's not reckless—it's self-aware.
- **Clients try to turn alternate rebellion into covert self-sabotage.**
  - → This is where gentle coaching comes in. If the behavior creates the same consequences as destructive rebellion, then it is not an alternate, and it's okay to call this out. Here you can help them problem-solve safer substitutions. The best way to utilize this skill (especially for highly impulsive clients) is to slow the process down and preplan options rather than choosing in the heat of the moment. Having a written list of preapproved alternate rebellious acts actually increases follow-through and reduces risky decision-making!
- **Clients say, "This is cheesy," "It sounds dumb," or "It won't help."**
  - → My response to this is often "Okay, I hear that. And are your current ways of rebelling working for you? Maybe it's dumb, but is it too dumb to try if it might actually help avoid negative consequences?" Give them the business a little bit here because even if it sounds dumb, it's still useful.

Alternate rebellion is most effective when it's taught with warmth, permission, and flexibility. Try to avoid moralizing or overstructuring this skill, because the more it feels like another rule, the less effective it becomes. When in doubt, ask yourself, "Does this help the client feel more autonomous and less likely to self-destruct?" If the answer is yes, you're doing it right!

Client Worksheet

Alternate Rebellion

How to rebel without burning your whole life down

Let's get one thing straight. Wanting to rebel does not mean there is something wrong with you. Some people are natural rule-followers, and some people are natural rebels. If you have a strong urge to push back, act out, fight against, or do the opposite of what you are told, that energy is *not* the problem. The problem is what happens when that rebellious energy comes out in ways that hurt you.

Alternate rebellion is a DBT skill that helps you express that rebellious part of you in ways that do not come with the same painful consequences. It is not about shutting down your rebellious side as much as it's about giving it a safer outlet.

Step 1: What Does Destructive Rebellion Look Like for You?

Think about how rebellion tends to show up in your life when it goes sideways. Examples might include substance use, self-harm, disordered eating, impulsive spending, blowing up relationships, skipping responsibilities, risky behaviors, or doing the opposite of what you know is good for you just to prove a point.

What are your most common destructive rebellious behaviors?

____

____

____

What usually triggers these urges for you? (Examples: feeling controlled, bored, invalidated, pressured, numb)

____

____

____

Step 2: What Are the Consequences of That Kind of Rebellion?

Be honest here. You want to notice patterns. When you've rebelled in the past in destructive ways, what happened after? What were the consequences?

____

____

____

____

Step 3: What Is Your Flavor of Alternate Rebellion?

Rebellion looks different for everyone. What feels rebellious to you might not feel rebellious to someone else. The goal is to find options that actually scratch that itch for you. The following are examples of alternate rebellion. These are meant to inspire you, not limit you. Put a check mark by anything that feels even a little interesting:

- ☐ Give an honest response instead of a polite one.
- ☐ Dye or cut your hair.
- ☐ Write a letter that you won't send expressing how you really feel.
- ☐ Explore new places.
- ☐ Say no when appropriate.
- ☐ Get a temporary tattoo.
- ☐ Get a real tattoo.
- ☐ Get a piercing.
- ☐ Go skinny dipping.
- ☐ Go to a nude beach.
- ☐ Blow off the work you have to do for the day.
- ☐ Talk in a phony accent to a complete stranger.
- ☐ Do something your parents would never let you do as a child.
- ☐ Wear your pajamas out in public.
- ☐ Wear a hat with a rebellious saying on it.
- ☐ Speak out rather than stay quiet.
- ☐ Wear clothes that speak to you regardless of whether you fit in.
- ☐ Dress in a unique and rebellious style.
- ☐ Wear really bright colors.
- ☐ Wear loud nail polish.
- ☐ Go to a late movie in the middle of the week.
- ☐ Do things out of character.
- ☐ Say no to a friend or family member when they ask for a favor.
- ☐ Dress up for a casual event or down for a fancy event.
- ☐ Take up a new rebellious hobby (e.g., tattooing, mountain biking).
- ☐ Wear shocking makeup.
- ☐ Challenge statements when you disagree.
- ☐ Yell out your window.
- ☐ Follow your passion rather than your expectation.
- ☐ Go to a "smash room" to break glass.
- ☐ Go axe throwing.
- ☐ Throw on your favorite rebellious music and play it as loud as you want.
- ☐ Run instead of walk.
- ☐ Turn up the volume.
- ☐ Roll down all the windows and blast your music.
- ☐ Play a different style of music.
- ☐ Leave things out of place or don't clean up when you normally would.
- ☐ Shout or scream alone.
- ☐ Sing super loud.
- ☐ Express unpopular views.
- ☐ Sleep late on the weekends or take a midday nap.
- ☐ Buy yourself something you want but have been holding off on.
- ☐ Buy something impractical just because.
- ☐ Do things out of order.
- ☐ Seek your own interests.

- ☐ Order in food instead of cooking.
- ☐ Cook something new and exciting.
- ☐ Be yourself with an attitude of "If you don't like it, don't look."
- ☐ Throw eggs outside.
- ☐ Throw ice in the bathtub.
- ☐ Get hair extensions.
- ☐ Have fun with new and different makeup.
- ☐ Go skydiving.
- ☐ Go rock climbing.
- ☐ Go to a thrilling and fun workout class.
- ☐ Book an impulsive trip.
- ☐ Visit a shooting range.
- ☐ Go skeet shooting.
- ☐ Play hooky.
- ☐ Break glass (safely!).
- ☐ Destroy old unneeded electronics (safely!).
- ☐ Play drums or other instruments loudly.
- ☐ Go to the batting cages.
- ☐ Take yourself on a date.
- ☐ Buy new clothes and create a new style or wardrobe.
- ☐ Other: ______________________
- ☐ Other: ______________________
- ☐ Other: ______________________

Step 4: Comparing Consequences

Now let's reality check this. Remember, you are not giving up rebellion. You are choosing rebellion that doesn't screw you over. Let's compare:

If you choose alternate rebellion instead of destructive rebellion, what do you think the consequences will be?

____

____

____

How might this safer form of rebellion give you the same satisfaction without the negative fallout?

____

____

____

Step 5: Making a Plan

Alternate rebellion works best when it's planned ahead of time, not chosen impulsively.

When you notice rebellious urges coming up, what can you try first?

____

____

____

Opposite Action

How to change your emotions by changing your behavior

Clients often assume the goal is to suppress or get rid of uncomfortable emotions. But plot twist! Emotions themselves are not the problem. Emotions are information. The problem is when emotions take the wheel and drive behavior in directions that make things worse for us. Opposite action offers an interesting third option: Clients can acknowledge the emotion and then choose a behavior that goes *against* the emotional urge when that urge is not helpful or effective (or maybe even harmful). It is deceptively simple and one of the most powerful ways to interrupt emotion-driven behavior.

This skill is especially helpful when emotions are intense, repetitive, and driving behaviors that create more suffering. Keep in mind that this isn't about denying feelings. It's about helping clients reduce the intensity and duration of painful emotions by changing what they do behaviorally. If you are at all familiar with AA or NA, it's similar to the concept of "move a muscle, change a thought." It's essentially saying behave differently, and that will make you feel differently.

The "why" behind opposite action is pretty straightforward and also twofold. First, acting on emotions often leads to destructive outcomes. Second, emotion-driven behaviors tend to intensify the very emotion that triggered them. Think about it like this: If you are angry and you punch a wall (anger = the emotion, punching a wall = emotion-driven behavior), your anger will likely increase afterward—not only are you still angry, but now you're also bloodied, bruised, and dealing with the consequences of your actions. Anger leads to lashing out, which strengths anger. Fear leads to avoidance, which strengthens fear. Sadness leads to withdrawal, which deepens sadness. Shame leads to hiding, which increases shame. It's a vicious cycle of feeling bad, acting on the feeling, and then feeling worse.

Opposite action works because behavior, whether we like it or not, sends powerful feedback to the brain. When we act *opposite* to an emotional urge, the brain gets new information that the situation may not be as dangerous, hopeless, or catastrophic as we first believed. Over time, this can soften emotional intensity and create more flexibility.

But do clients always need to use opposite action when they have painful emotions? And how do they decide when it's appropriate to use it?

Here's the answer: Opposite action is 100 percent appropriate when the emotion-driven behavior is harmful. For example, if someone is going through a breakup and feels intense rejection, their emotion-driven behavior might be to self-harm by cutting their arms. That's clearly harmful, so they'd want to practice opposite action to offset the intensity of the emotion and prevent the maladaptive behavior. Now, if a client says they are feeling rejected after a breakup and the emotion-driven behavior is to sit on the couch, cry to *Bridget Jones's Diary*, and eat some ice cream, then no, I would not say that opposite action is needed. Some emotions (even painful ones) are okay to sit through as long as the behavior that comes with them isn't harmful.

Teaching the Skill in Session

As always, lead with validation. Let clients know that their emotions are valid and understandable, even when they are painful! You can also emphasize that opposite action is not emotional avoidance as much as it is regulation. I often explain it as "You're allowed to feel exactly how you feel. You're just not required to obey the feeling." Then you can break the skill down into five steps that feel manageable rather than overwhelming.

Step 1: Identify and Rate the Emotion

Help the client name the emotion and rate its intensity on the SUDs scale. Naming the emotion slows things down and increases awareness.

Step 2: Identify Typical Emotion-Driven Behaviors

Ask the client what they typically do when they experience this emotion. Encourage specificity here—vague answers like "I shut down" are less helpful than concrete behaviors like isolating, skipping meals, avoiding emails, or snapping at people.

Step 3: Assess the Need for Opposite Action

Determine whether those behaviors are effective and whether opposite action is necessary. Gently but directly link the emotion-driven behavior to its outcomes. If the behavior is creating more distress or causing harm, it's time to use opposite action.

Step 4: Plan a Concrete Opposite Action

Collaboratively identify what the opposite action would look like. Make it concrete and observable. For example, "Be nicer" is not an opposite action, but "Lower my voice and pause before responding" is. Remember, opposite action lives on a spectrum, so if your client is feeling 9/10 depressed and their emotion-driven behavior is to isolate and not shower for days, the "perfect opposite" (e.g., socializing, having spa day, going out on the town) is unrealistic. Sometimes the opposite action might be to call someone for five minutes, take a quick shower, and open the windows to get fresh air. Think "doable" over "the most opposite." In addition, have the client do the opposite action for a specific, realistic window of time rather than forever. This lowers resistance and increases follow-through.

Step 5: Monitor Emotions

After the opposite action is completed, check where the client is now on the SUDs scale. Even a small shift is a win! If there's no change, that's okay too. It's just an indication that another skill could be used here or a different opposite action.

Emotion-Specific Coaching Examples

Anger

- **Emotion-driven behavior:** attacking, criticizing, yelling, ruminating
- **Opposite action:** stepping away, softening tone, validating, acknowledging personal responsibility

Anxiety

- **Emotion-driven behavior:** avoidance, withdrawal
- **Opposite action:** approaching what is feared, doing the thing that scares you, moving closer in small, planned steps

Sadness

- **Emotion-driven behavior:** isolation, staying in bed, rumination, passivity
- **Opposite action:** practicing gentle self-care, scheduling activities, connecting with others, engaging in something mildly pleasant or meaningful

Guilt or Shame

- **Emotion-driven behavior:** hiding, self-punishment, withdrawal, or overapologizing
- **Opposite action:** seeking support, practicing self-compassion, repairing when appropriate, staying visible instead of disappearing

Addressing Common Client Pitfalls

It's normal for clients to resist or question opposite action at first. Here are a few common concerns and how to address them:

- **Clients say, "This feels fake" or "I don't feel like doing the opposite."**
  - → That makes sense! Opposite action is effortful by design. You can normalize this by reminding clients that the goal is not to feel motivated first—motivation often comes *after* behavior, not before it.
- **Clients worry that opposite action means ignoring their emotions.**
  - → This is where it is important to reiterate that they always acknowledge the emotion first. They aren't ignoring or denying how they feel. They are very much in touch with their emotions and validating them, *and* they're intentionally choosing their behavior so they can respond strategically.

Something to keep in mind both for you and your clients: Opposite action is not a one-and-done skill. It tends to work best when practiced repeatedly and reviewed reflectively in sessions. What I like to do is encourage clients to notice even small shifts in emotional intensity rather than expecting full relief. That expectation shift can help avoid disappointment when their emotions don't totally dissipate with opposite action. *Remember, emotional regulation, not emotional elimination!*

Client Worksheet

Opposite Action

How to change your emotions by changing your behavior

Opposite action is a skill you use when your emotions are real and valid, but the behaviors they drive are making things worse. This skill helps you acknowledge the emotion without letting it show. To be clear, you are not wrong for having emotions. You are just learning how to respond to them differently.

Step 1: Name the Emotion

Think of a situation that tends to trigger a strong emotional response in you—one that often leads to harmful, unhelpful, or risky behavior. What emotion do you normally feel in that situation? (Examples: anger, anxiety, sadness, shame, guilt, fear)

____

____

On a scale of 0–10, how intense does that emotion feel when you are in that situation?

SUDs: _____ / 10

Step 2: Notice the Urge

When this intense emotion shows up, what does it usually push you to do? Try to be specific and concrete. (Examples: isolating, snapping at someone, avoiding responsibilities, engaging in self-harm)

____

____

Step 3: Is Acting on This Emotion Helping or Hurting?

Take a moment to zoom out. When you act on these urges, what usually happens afterward?

Short-term relief (if any):

____

____

Long-term consequences or fallout:

____

____

Based on this, does acting on this emotion move you closer to the life you want or farther away?

☐ Closer ☐ Farther

Step 4: Decide If Opposite Action Is Needed

Opposite action is helpful when the emotion-driven behavior is harmful, is ineffective, or keeps you stuck. With that in mind, do you think opposite action would be a good fit for this situation?

☐ Yes ☐ No ☐ Not sure yet

If you answered no or not sure, what approach feels more helpful right now?

____

____

Step 5: Choose Your Opposite Action

If you are using opposite action, the goal is not to do the biggest or hardest opposite. It's to do something realistic and doable. Thinking about the emotional urges you listed in step 2, what is a small, realistic opposite behavior you could try instead the next time the situation comes up?

____

____

How long are you willing to try this opposite action for? (Examples: five minutes, ten minutes, one conversation, one task)

____

____

Step 6: Check Back In

After trying the opposite action, pause and reassess. On a scale of 0–10, how intense does that emotion feel right now?

SUDs: ______ / 10

Did anything shift, even a little?

☐ Yes ☐ No ☐ Not sure

What did you notice?

____

____

Sometimes the emotion softens, and sometimes it stays the same. Either way, you practiced a skill and that still counts! Progress here is about emotional regulation, not emotion elimination.

Checking the Facts

How to separate what actually happened from the story the brain tells about it

Checking the facts is a core emotion regulation skill that helps slow down emotionally driven interpretations and reality check the assumptions that that fuel distress and overwhelm. It's especially helpful for clients who experience emotions that feel sudden, intense, and convincing—often based on partial information or filtered thinking. (Which, by the way, is incredibly human!) I once heard a quote that went something like this: "The core of our emotional dysregulation isn't about what happened; it's about the story we tell ourselves about what happened."

In that same spirit, checking the facts helps us answer one deceptively simple question: "Does the intensity of my emotion fit the actual facts of the situation?" Checking the facts is not about gaslighting ourselves, invalidating emotions, or forcing positive thinking. It's all about gently identifying when an emotional reaction is being driven by our perception of events, rather than by objective reality. A useful way to frame this for clients is to explain that our emotions are real, but they are not always accurate reporters of facts. Emotions respond to our *interpretation* of events, not the events themselves. When that interpretation is incomplete, filtered, or distorted, emotions can skyrocket unnecessarily. Here are some examples of what unchecked interpretations often sound like:

- "They hate me."
- "I messed everything up."
- "This always happens to me."
- "No one cares."
- "I'm a failure."
- "I'll never be okay."

What we want to avoid is treating these interpretations as facts without examining the evidence. By checking the facts, clients can learn to pause, gather information, and widen their lens before responding. Think of it as being an ethical researcher. If you were running a study, you'd start with a hypothesis on how you think things might shake out, right? That's what all scientists do. But a careful scientist doesn't just look for evidence that supports their hypothesis—they also look for evidence that contradicts it. That's how balanced and realistic conclusions are drawn. You want clients to take that same approach to their own lives.

Since clients often fear that this skill means their feelings are "wrong," I make sure to emphasize that their emotion makes sense based on the story their brain told them. With this skill, we are simply checking whether that story is the full picture. I like to frame it as curiosity rather than correction. Clients aren't asking, "Is this thought wrong?" They're asking, "What information am I using, and what info might I be missing here?"

It's also helpful to clearly separate the situation from their interpretation, as many clients will initially blur these together. Gently remind them that facts are observable and verifiable, while interpretations are conclusions about meaning or intent. For example, "They didn't text me back for six hours" is factual, whereas "They're mad at me and pulling away" is an *interpretation* of that fact. Helping clients make this distinction is often where the biggest insight happens!

Addressing Common Client Pitfalls

Even with clear guidance, clients can sometimes get stuck or misunderstand this skill. Here are a few common challenges and how to respond to them:

- **Clients confuse emotional evidence with factual evidence, saying things like "It feels true" or "I just know."**
  - → Those tidbits are important emotional data, but they are not objective facts. I like to gently challenge this by saying, "I get it, you feel how you feel, but if you were an unbiased party just watching what's happening, not interpreting it, what would you see, objectively?"
- **Clients use checking the facts to invalidate themselves.**
  - → If a client quickly jumps to "I'm overreacting" or "I shouldn't feel this way," slow them down a bit. The goal is never to shame the emotion away because it's likely that this client has been reinforcing this narrative for a long, long time. It's very possible this narrative was even dictated by others in their lives, reinforcing it tenfold. The goal is not to shame the emotions, but to understand what is driving them.
- **Clients struggle to generate alternative explanations.**
  - → In these moments, collaborative brainstorming can be helpful. It's your job to offer some neutral possibilities rather than overly positive ones to keep the exercise grounded and believable. You aren't going for toxic positivity here. Just neutrality to take the sting out.

When the Facts Are Accurate (and Still Hurt)

Brace yourself for a hard truth: Sometimes clients check the facts and realize that the facts are actually true. For example, a client may feel unlovable because they say they've never been in a romantic relationship, and when they check the facts, it is objectively true that they have never been in a relationship. This can feel discouraging or even invalidating if you are not skillful in how you frame the skill.

Checking the facts is not meant to prove the client wrong or make painful emotions disappear. Its purpose is to separate what is factual from the meaning the brain assigns to those facts. The fact may be "I have never been in a relationship." The interpretation layered on top ("That means I am unlovable") is not a fact; it is a conclusion. When this happens, remember to lead with validation. It makes sense to feel sad, lonely, or discouraged when a real desire for connection has not been met. That emotional response fits the facts. What does not automatically follow, however, is a global belief about the client's worth, lovability, or future.

In this case, you might explore the idea that instead of concluding "I'm unlovable," another neutral interpretation could be that their life simply has not included a romantic relationship yet. This says more about timing and experience than their personal worth. This is a painful and valid longing, but it's not evidence that something is wrong with them.

As a heads-up, it's possible (even likely) that even after checking the facts, clients may still feel hurt, anxious, or disappointed. This is a great place to reinforce realistic expectations. A shift from an 8 to a 5 on the SUDs scale is still meaningful progress! Noticing even small changes reinforces the effectiveness of the skill and reduces all-or-nothing thinking.

Checking the Facts

How to separate what actually happened from the story the brain tells about it

When your emotions feel intense or overwhelming, it is often because your brain filled in missing pieces with assumptions, interpretations, or worst-case scenarios. Very annoying, but true. Checking the facts helps you slow things down and take a deeper look at what actually happened versus what you told yourself it meant.

This skill isn't about proving yourself wrong or invalidating how you feel as much as it is about understanding what is driving the emotion so you can respond more skillfully.

Step 1: What Happened?

First, describe the situation that triggered the emotional reaction. Stick to just the observable facts (e.g., "They told me they needed to hang up the phone" versus "They were annoyed with me"). Imagine a video camera recording the moment.

____

____

Step 2: What Did Your Brain Say About It?

Now notice the thoughts, interpretations, or conclusions that showed up. What did you tell yourself that this situation meant?

____

____

Step 3: What Emotion Did That Create?

What emotion came up for you in response to that interpretation? It's okay if there are multiple.

____

____

On a scale of 0–10, how intense does that emotion feel when you are in that situation?

SUDs: ______ / 10

Step 4: What Is the Objective Evidence?

Look at the facts again, like an unbiased observer. What evidence supports your interpretation? What evidence might contradict or complicate it?

____

____

Step 5: Are There Other Possible Explanations?

You are not looking for overly positive explanations, just realistic or neutral ones. What are one or two neutral alternative explanations?

____

____

Step 6: Revisit the Meaning

Based on *all* the information, how might you revise your original interpretation?

Original interpretation:

____

____

Revised or more balanced interpretation:

____

____

Step 7: Check Back In Emotionally

After checking the facts, how intense does the emotion feel now?

SUDs: ______ / 10

Did anything shift, even slightly?

☐ Yes ☐ No ☐ Not sure

What do you notice now?

____

____

Sometimes the facts are real and still painful. Checking the facts does not necessarily erase your pain, but it can help prevent additional suffering by stopping painful situations from turning into a party of self-blame, shame, or global conclusions about who you are.

Problem-Solving

How to take skillful action when a problem can actually be solved

Emotions often escalate when we feel powerless, stuck, or unsure of what to do next. Even when our emotions absolutely fit the facts of a situation, suffering increases when we have no sense of agency and feel like there's nothing we can do to feel better. Problem-solving helps restore that sense of agency by breaking an overwhelming situation into manageable, concrete steps. It is most appropriate when a situation is actually changeable and when the emotion we are experiencing fits the facts of that situation.

Unlike some DBT skills, which help clients tolerate pain or regulate emotional intensity, problem-solving answers a different question: "Is there something I can actually do about this?" It replaces "I don't know what to do" with "Here's my next small step." This is especially empowering for clients who spiral into overthinking, catastrophizing, or helplessness, as they often get stuck oscillating between emotional overwhelm and inaction. This is a totally normal human reaction, especially when folks have not been taught how to effectively work through life's difficulties. Problem-solving provides a pathway out of that rumination and toward purposeful action, one step at a time.

Teaching point: Problem-solving is not about fixing emotions directly, but recognizing that emotions tend to soften as a byproduct of effective action.

When to Use (and Not Use) Problem-Solving

Before introducing this skill to clients, it is crucial to assess whether problem-solving is even the right move. Problem-solving is the vibe when:

- The problem is within the client's control to influence.
- The emotion fits the facts of the situation.
- Action is possible and appropriate.

Problem-solving is not the vibe when:

- The situation is unchangeable.
- The client is emotionally flooded and outside their TLA.
- The client is using problem-solving to avoid feeling something they need to feel.

In those moments, distress tolerance, radical acceptance, or self-compassion may need to come first. Sometimes, a situation isn't changeable and problem-solving isn't the answer. Think of this as a tool when the problem actually has some flexibility, not as a magic wand for every messy feeling.

Steps to Problem-Solving

When you introduce this skill to clients, normalize that overwhelm makes thinking harder. When they're dysregulated, the frontal lobe tends to get flooded, and it doesn't fire on all cylinders. Therefore, even if they *know* that their problem is solvable, the emotional intensity makes it hard to work out cognitively. The accompanying client-facing worksheet is intentionally structured to externalize thinking so clients don't have to hold everything in their head at once.

The first step of this skill—identifying the problem—is often where you need to slow clients down a bit. Many clients describe problems vaguely or emotionally, so you'll want to guide them toward more specificity. What is actually happening? Who is involved? What is or isn't occurring? You know what they say: A well-defined problem is half-solved!

The next step is to identify goals. This is where you want to help clients focus on goals that are realistic and emotion focused rather than outcome-perfect. Goals like "I want to feel safer" or "I want less stress" are more workable than "I want everything to be fixed." From there, help clients brainstorm possible solutions before choosing one to try. When selecting a solution, encourage clients to prioritize what feels doable over what feels ideal. If a solution feels overwhelming, simplify even further until it feels doable for them!

Finally, break the plan down into concrete action steps. This is where the *magic* happens. It's where overwhelm turns into movement, stuckness into action, and powerlessness into empowerment. Encourage clients to write out steps so small that they almost feel silly. That is usually the right size when someone is overwhelmed and trying to move forward.

Addressing Common Client Pitfalls

On paper, problem-solving can seem simple and straightforward. In real life, it rarely is. Here are some common ways clients can get tripped up and how you can address them:

- **Clients try to problem-solve situations that are not actually theirs to solve, such as other people's feelings or behaviors.**
  - → Remind clients that trying to solve someone else's experience often increases frustration rather than reducing it. Gently redirect them toward what is within their locus of control.
- **Clients rush through the worksheet intellectually without the emotional buy-in.**
  - → Slow the process down and reconnect to why the problem matters emotionally and how addressing it could bring them some relief. If they stay purely analytical, they may not internalize the work.
- **Clients believe they're a failure if the solution they pick doesn't work.**
  - → A solution that doesn't work is *not* a sign of failure. Normalize that most problems require more than one attempt or approach. Plan B is not a sign of defeat, and neither is plan C! This is just a part of effective problem-solving. The troubleshooting step reinforces flexibility and persistence rather than all-or-nothing thinking.

- **Clients use problem-solving prematurely to escape discomfort.**
  → When someone is flooded with emotion, their brain is in survival mode, not solution mode. In that state, problem-solving tends to become reactive rather than actually addressing the situation. Therefore, if a client's emotions are too intense, pause and pivot to emotion regulation strategies first, such as grounding, paced breathing, or self-soothing. Once their emotional temperature comes down to a manageable level, their thinking brain can reengage, and problem-solving becomes much more effective.

Client Worksheet

Problem-Solving

How to take skillful action when a problem can actually be solved

Problem-solving is a skill you can use when a problem in your life is changeable, and taking action can help reduce your emotional suffering. Some problems have solutions, and if you can flex that muscle, why not? This skill is about breaking a problem down so it feels more manageable instead of paralyzing. Know that you do not have to solve all your problems today, though. You just have to take the next right step—and even small movement is still movement, my friend!

Step 1: Identify the Problem

Describe the problem as clearly and specifically as you can. Try to stick to what is actually happening rather than how upsetting it feels.

What is the problem?

____

____

____

Who is involved?

____

____

____

What is happening or not happening?

____

____

____

Step 2: Identify Your Goal

What would you like to change about this situation? What would help you feel even a little better emotionally? Identify your goal here.

____

____

____

Step 3: Brainstorm Possible Solutions

List as many possible solutions as you can. Go wild! There are no right answers here. The goal is to widen your options, not to pick the perfect solution. Try to list at least three possible solutions.

Step 4: Choose One Solution to Try First

What solution will you try first? Know that you are not committing to this solution forever. You are just choosing one option to experiment with.

Why does this solution feel most doable right now?

Step 5: Break It Down into Action Steps

Now make the plan realistic! Break your chosen solution down into the smallest possible actions. If a step feels overwhelming, make it even smaller until it feels doable.

1.
2.
3.
4.
5.
6.

Step 6: Try It Out

Take the steps you listed in step 5. You do not need to do them perfectly—you just need to try.

When will you start?

____

____

____

Step 7: Troubleshooting (If Needed)

If this solution does not work, that does not mean you failed. It just means you gathered information and you can try plans B, C, or D. That's why you wrote out several possible options!

What worked?

____

____

____

What did not work?

____

____

____

Behavioral Chain Analysis

How to slow down emotional chaos and understand why a behavior happened

Behavioral chain analysis is a *chef's kiss* of a DBT skill for helping clients understand their behaviors without shame, self-blame, or oversimplified explanations like "I'm just broken" or "I always mess things up." At its core, a chain analysis helps clients see that maladaptive behaviors don't just come out of nowhere. They aren't bad luck, uncontrollable flukes, or totally helpless things that happen to us. They are constructed patterns, step by step. Link by link.

When clients engage in unhelpful behaviors—whether it's bingeing, self-harm, impulsive texting, substance use, emotional outbursts, avoidance, people-pleasing, shutting down—there is *always* a sequence of internal and external events that led them there. Even when the symptoms feel like they hit out of nowhere, there is always a pattern to be seen. The behavior makes sense when you zoom out—and a chain analysis is how we do that.

I often tell clients that a behavior chain is like rewinding the tape. Instead of only zooming in on the moment they "messed up," they're slowing the tape down and asking, "What was happening before this? What was already making things harder? What thoughts and feelings were quietly stacking up? And where could I have intervened earlier?" For anyone who played sports in high school, this is literally watching a game tape!

This skill lives in emotion regulation for a reason because understanding the chain that led up to certain behaviors can reduce shame, increase insight, and create actual points of change. Not hypothetical change. Real, practical, skill-based change that feels more workable and frees clients from feeling stuck and like "nothing will ever change."

The "Why" Behind Behavioral Chain Analysis

Most clients come into therapy laser focused on the behavior they regret. They want to stop it, fix it, or erase it—all completely fair. But if they only focus on the end of the chain, they miss the real leverage points that actually help curb behavior.

The beauty of behavioral chain analysis is that it teaches clients that change does not happen only at the last step. Instead, the earlier the intervention, the easier the behavior is to shift. It is much easier to eat a snack when you are tired and hungry than it is to resist a binge urge that's hitting at a 9 out of 10 intensity. It is much easier to cope skillfully with sadness than it is to undo a rage text that already got sent.

This skill also gently dismantles the idea that people choose behaviors out of nowhere or because they lack willpower. Instead, it illustrates how vulnerabilities, triggers, thoughts, emotions, and urges interact and lead to unwanted behaviors. And to be honest, that insight alone is often incredibly validating and regulating!

How to Walk Through the Chain

Many clients feel embarrassed or exposed walking through the chain, but this is an excellent opportunity to let them know that their discomfort is totally common and temporary, and that clarity almost always brings some relief. I frame this skill as detective work, not self-criticism. Clients are not on trial. They are simply gathering data. The goal here is not to judge themselves, but to understand themselves more thoroughly. If clients want different outcomes, they need to understand the full story of how they got to where they are. Here are the steps to completing a behavioral chain:

Step 1: Start with Vulnerabilities

Identify the factors that increased the client's emotional vulnerability. Examples include being tired, hungry, sick, lonely, stressed, overstimulated, undersupported, or emotionally raw. This is where clients often have light bulb moments, and understandably so!

Step 2: Identify the Prompting Event

This is the specific trigger that set the chain in motion. Help clients be precise here—not "My whole day sucked," but "My boss criticized my work in a meeting" or "My partner didn't text me back for hours."

Step 3: Explore Associated Emotions and Thoughts

Gently ask about the underlying emotions and thoughts that accompanied this prompting event. This is where core beliefs show up quietly and powerfully. You might hear something like "Because my partner did not text back for hours, I felt angry and rejected. I thought 'He's going to leave me.'" I strongly encourage you to slow this part down as best as possible. Clients often rush past their internal experiences or default to only one common surface emotion.

Step 4: Explore Associated Urges

Ask clients what they felt the urge to do in response to these thoughts and emotions. This is a critical pivot point! Urges are not actions yet. In DBT, we distinguish between urges (which pull the body and brain toward relief) versus the behavior itself. Helping clients recognize this distinction can increase their sense of agency and open the door for skill use. And most importantly, it opens a pause between "I have the urge to do _____" and actually doing it.

Step 5: Identify the Behavior Itself

Keep this factual and nonjudgmental. Just describe what happened without overidentifying. Instead of "I acted like an idiot," the client might say, "I sent seven angry texts in a row."

Step 6: Explore the Consequences, Both Short Term and Long Term

Look at what the behavior did immediately versus over time. Often, behavior makes sense in the short term but causes problems in the long term. Naming both sides reduces black-and-white thinking and helps clients understand why the behavior keeps happening.

Step 7: Move Into Solutions

Once the chain is laid out and the client can see the full sequence of events, go back through each link in the chain and ask, "What skills could you apply next time to break the chain?" You are trying to identify realistic points of intervention across each link in the chain. Earlier intervention points are usually easier and more sustainable than last-minute crisis skills, but all options matter! Treat it like you are John Madden going back over a play postgame.

> **Encourage flexibility:** Not every chain needs to be filled out perfectly! This is for the Virgo clients and the perfectionists. Sometimes the goal is insight, sometimes pattern recognition, and sometimes prevention planning. Rock with it whatever it is.

Addressing Common Client Pitfalls

Chain analysis can bring up resistance, shame, or the urge to rush. While that's normal, here is how to navigate these common reactions:

- **Clients say, "This feels like overthinking," or "I already know why I do this."**
  → Gently remind them that knowing something in theory is (annoyingly) much different from mapping it concretely. The chain makes the invisible visible.
- **Clients jump straight to solutions.**
  → Slow them down. If clients don't fully understand the chain, the solutions they come up with will tend to be vague and ineffective. The more precise the chain, the more targeted the intervention.
- **Clients get stuck in shame.**
  → Encourage curiosity, shifting from "What's wrong with me?" to "What actually happened here?" The point isn't to get upset, but to get curious. Perhaps it's silly, but I like to ask clients to step into the role of a clinician so they can look at the chain objectively—it can feel surprisingly empowering for them. Most importantly, do your best to model compassion. When you approach the chain with curiosity and warmth, clients learn to do the same for themselves. And that is often just as therapeutic as the behavior change itself!

Behavioral chain analysis is very much not a one-and-done skill. The more clients practice it, the faster and more intuitive it becomes. Over time, many clients will actually start doing mini-chain analyses in their heads in real time, which is what we're aiming for! Again, think Neo in *The Matrix* dodging slow-moving bullets because of his next-level awareness. Pretty badass, if you ask me.

Behavioral Chain Analysis

How to slow down emotional chaos and understand why a behavior happened

The goal of this worksheet is not to judge, criticize, or label yourself as "bad." It's to understand and gain insight into your behaviors. When you understand how a behavior happened, you give yourself more options to handle it strategically next time. Think of this like rewinding the tape. You're trying to slow everything way down so you can see the full picture of what actually led up to a behavior you want to change. Behaviors don't come out of nowhere—they are often built on patterns. And here's the kicker: If something was built, it can also be changed!

Step 1: Vulnerabilities

What was already making things harder before the situation even happened?

Vulnerabilities are anything that lowered your emotional resilience before the chain started. For example, you might have been tired, hungry, sick, stressed, overwhelmed, lonely, overstimulated, undersupported, emotionally raw, or insecure.

What vulnerabilities were present for you?

____

____

Step 2: The Prompting Event

What actually happened that kicked this whole thing off?

This is the specific event that triggered the chain. Try to be concrete and factual here. Think what a video camera would have captured about the event—not your interpretations or assumptions about it. For example, instead of "My whole day sucked," aim for something like "My boss criticized my work in a meeting" or "My partner didn't text me back for several hours."

What was the prompting event?

____

____

Step 3: Thoughts and Emotions

What went on inside you after the prompting event?

Slow this part down as much as you can. Often, there's a more obvious emotion on the surface and then a deeper, more vulnerable one underneath. There are also usually thoughts or beliefs that show up alongside the emotions. Try to name both the emotions and thoughts you noticed.

What surface emotions did you notice?

____

____

What underlying emotions were present (if any)?

____

____

What thoughts, interpretations, or self-talk showed up in your mind at the time?

____

____

Step 4: Urges

What did those thoughts and feelings pull you toward wanting to do?

Reminder: Urges are not actions. They are a pull toward relief. This is an important moment of choice in the chain, even if it doesn't feel like one at the time.

What urges did you notice?

____

____

Step 5: The Behavior

What did you actually do?

This is the behavior you're looking to understand or change. Keep this part factual and nonjudgmental. Be gentle with yourself here. No labels. No commentary. Just describe what happened.

What behavior did you engage in?

____

____

Step 6: Consequences

What happened after the behavior?

Most behaviors "work" in the short term and cost you in the long term. Both matter.

In the short term, what did you gain or experience for engaging in the behavior?

____

____

In the long term, what did this behavior cost you or create more of?

____

____

Did any of these consequences create new vulnerabilities or feed back into the cycle?

____

____

Step 7: Breaking the Chain

Where could you intervene next time?

Now that you can see the full chain from a bird's-eye view, go back through it and look for places where things could shift next time. You don't need to change everything. Even just a single different choice can change the outcome!

At the vulnerability stage, what might help reduce risk next time?

____

____

At the prompting event stage, what skills or supports could help?

____

____

When difficult thoughts or emotions show up, what skills could help you respond differently?

____

____

When urges hit, what could help you pause or ride the wave?

If needed, what skills could help you cope with consequences more effectively?

Final Reflection

What stands out to you after doing this chain, if anything? You might notice some patterns. You might feel relief. You might feel annoyed. All of this is okay! This is just data to learn more about yourself.

What did you learn about yourself from this exercise?

Building Mastery

How doing small, skillful things builds emotional stability and self-trust

Building mastery is one of those DBT skills that looks deceptively simple and then quietly changes people's lives. It's not flashy. It doesn't promise instant relief. But over time, it does something incredibly important for emotional regulation. It helps clients build evidence that they are capable, competent, and able to do hard things. On the surface, it seems like this skill just involves doing hobbies, but trust me, this one is a good one.

What Building Mastery Is (and Is Not)

Building mastery is about intentionally engaging in (fun!) activities that create a sense of accomplishment. Disclaimer, this is not about being productive, impressing others, or turning hobbies into side hustles or monetizing joy. That distinction matters, especially for high-achieving or perfectionistic clients who tend to tie their self-worth to outcomes. (And I've been stuck there myself, so I get it!)

This is also not about perfection. Mistakes, frustration, and learning curves are part of the process. In fact, tolerating imperfection is often where the mastery actually happens. It's not about mastery in the "expert" sense. It's about doing things that stretch clients just enough to require a bit of effort, leaving them with that subtle but powerful feeling of "I did that." I like to frame it as "confidence built from the inside out." The goal isn't to find their lifelong passion or become amazing at something overnight. It's all about choosing activities that are just challenging enough to require effort, but not so hard that they feel overwhelming or impossible.

This skill is especially helpful for folks who struggle with low self-esteem, chronic shame, emotional fragility, or a persistent sense of inadequacy. Many of these clients are stuck in a loop of emotional dysregulation that quietly erodes their confidence—it's very insidious and slow, but nonetheless there. When emotions run the show, their behaviors shrink, and clients tend to avoid or disengage. They stop trying new things, and over time, this avoidance reinforces the belief that they are incapable or broken.

Building mastery directly interrupts that cycle. By engaging in small, achievable activities that require effort and practice, clients start collecting evidence against those negative beliefs. Each completed task, each skill practiced, each small win becomes data for them. And that data is more powerful than you might think. Over time, these experiences accumulate and create a more stable sense of self-worth that is not dependent on mood, validation, or external approval. I often explain this skill as emotional compound interest. One small deposit does not change much. But repeated deposits over time create real stability!

It can be helpful to normalize that this skill may feel boring, pointless, or even annoying at first. Many clients expect emotional regulation to come from insight, processing, or talking things out. In contrast, this skill asks them to regulate their emotions by *doing*. For some, that shift can feel uncomfortable, especially if they are used to intellectualizing their way through their distress. I like to explain, "We're not doing this to distract you or keep you busy. We're doing this to slowly rebuild trust in yourself that you are a capable human being. It's about becoming someone who follows through, even in small ways."

How to Build Mastery

Start by helping clients identify activities that genuinely spark their interest or align with their values. If the activity feels forced or performative, it will not work. Then encourage them to start small—very small. The biggest pitfall with building mastery is setting goals that are too big, too vague, or too emotionally loaded. You want low-risk, low-pressure activities that still require engagement but stretch them just enough to feel satisfying and meaningful. The key is to integrate these activities into the client's life in a way that feels natural and aligned with who they are. It does not need to be flashy to be effective. In fact, the quieter the win, the more powerful it often becomes.

In addition, encourage consistency over intensity. Five minutes of practice done regularly will do way more for emotional regulation than a single burst of overly ambitious effort that quickly burns out. Mastery is built through repetition, not intensity. Progress counts. Effort counts. Showing up counts. And yes, hobbies absolutely count!

It's also important to make space to celebrate the client's progress. Many clients automatically dismiss small wins, but taking a moment to notice what they accomplished, how it felt, and what it says about their capabilities reinforces the value of their effort. Finally, help clients tie mastery back to emotional regulation. Point out that by engaging in mastery-building activities, they'll feel more stable, confident, or resilient over time. This helps the skill feel purposeful rather than arbitrary. They begin to see themselves as someone who practices, tries, learns, and grows. And that shift alone can significantly reduce emotional vulnerability.

Addressing Common Client Pitfalls

When teaching this skill, don't be surprised if you encounter resistance, confusion, or self-criticism from clients. Here's how to address these common pitfalls like a pro.

- **Clients say, "This feels pointless" or "How is this supposed to help my emotions?"**
  - → This is a great moment for psychoeducation and patience. Remind clients that building mastery works gradually, not immediately. It's a long game! Emphasize that small, consistent progress will slowly build their confidence and resilience over time.
- **Clients turn this skill into another area of self-criticism.**
  - → Enter perfectionists! If clients miss a day or struggle with an activity, they may label themselves as failures. This is where you gently redirect them back to self-compassion and flexibility. Reinforce that the goal is engagement, not perfection, and that showing up (even imperfectly!) counts as progress.

- **Clients choose activities that are either too easy or too overwhelming.**
  - → Both extremes will limit the effectiveness of this skill. Help them calibrate by aiming for activities that are "challenging but doable." If a task feels too easy, nudge them so it requires more effort. It if feels too overwhelming, break into something simpler.

Client Worksheet

Building Mastery

How doing small, skillful things builds emotional stability and self-trust

Building mastery is about doing small things that help you feel capable and competent. Not perfect and not impressive, just capable. Over time, these small experiences will add up and help steady your emotions, build your self-trust, and quiet that voice of shame or inadequacy. This worksheet is meant to help you intentionally choose activities that stretch you just enough to create that "I did that" proud feeling.

Step 1: What Does Mastery Mean for You?

When you imagine feeling more capable or confident in your life, what comes to mind? This does not have to be big or dramatic. Think small, realistic, and personal.

____

____

Step 2: Choose a Building Mastery Activity

Building mastery works best when you do an activity you actually enjoy or feel curious about. It should require some effort, but not so much that you immediately shut down if you don't get it right off the jump. The following is a list of real, practical ideas. Check off any that feel like a good place to start. You don't need to love them. You just need to be willing to try one if it sounds slightly interesting.

Everyday Life and Home

- ☐ Making your bed consistently
- ☐ Organizing one drawer or small space
- ☐ Cooking one simple meal without rushing
- ☐ Trying a new recipe
- ☐ Baking something basic
- ☐ Cleaning one area thoroughly
- ☐ Doing laundry from start to finish in one go
- ☐ Meal planning for a few days
- ☐ Grocery shopping with a list
- ☐ Decorating or rearranging a space
- ☐ Doing a small home project
- ☐ Learning how to fix something minor

Creative and Hands-On

- ☐ Drawing, doodling, or sketching
- ☐ Painting or using watercolors
- ☐ Knitting, crocheting, or sewing
- ☐ Making pottery or ceramics
- ☐ Sculpting with clay
- ☐ Creating DIY crafts or art projects
- ☐ Arranging flowers
- ☐ Taking or editing photos
- ☐ Journaling or writing
- ☐ Exploring creative writing or poetry
- ☐ Scrapbooking
- ☐ Designing something digitally
- ☐ Building miniatures or models

Learning and Skill Building

- ☐ Learning a new language (even casually)
- ☐ Practicing vocabulary
- ☐ Taking an online class
- ☐ Learning a new app or software
- ☐ Learning basic coding
- ☐ Improving your typing speed
- ☐ Studying a topic you're curious about
- ☐ Learning to read music
- ☐ Learning to play an instrument
- ☐ Practicing chess or strategy games
- ☐ Leveling up on a new video game

Movement and Body-Based

- ☐ Doing yoga or Pilates
- ☐ Stretching
- ☐ Walking with intention
- ☐ Hiking
- ☐ Dancing
- ☐ Learning choreography
- ☐ Playing a sport
- ☐ Practicing balance or flexibility
- ☐ Strength training

Mental and Cognitive

- ☐ Doing crossword puzzles
- ☐ Playing word games
- ☐ Doing brainteasers
- ☐ Playing sudoku
- ☐ Doing puzzles
- ☐ Playing memory games
- ☐ Reading regularly
- ☐ Listening to audiobooks
- ☐ Meditating

Social and Real-World Skills

- ☐ Practicing public speaking
- ☐ Planning a small event
- ☐ Hosting a dinner or gathering
- ☐ Giving thoughtful gifts
- ☐ Planning a vacation
- ☐ Thrifting intentionally
- ☐ Selling or organizing items you've collected
- ☐ Blogging or vlogging
- ☐ Joining a class or group
- ☐ Practicing assertive communication

Step 3: Start Small on Purpose

The goal is not to do this perfectly. The goal is to do it consistently. What is a small, realistic version of this activity you can commit to? Think five minutes, not an hour. Once or twice a week instead of every day.

____

____

Step 4: Practice and Notice

Building mastery is an emotion regulation skill, so you want to connect the dots. Each time you engage in this activity, pause afterward and notice how it feels. Even if it was frustrating or imperfect, you still showed up—and that counts. After doing the activity, what did you notice? Did you notice any shift in your mood, confidence, or self-talk?

____

____

Step 5: Reflect on Progress (Not Perfection)

Remember that you don't need to do this every day! You don't even need to be good at it. You just need to keep coming back and trying. What does following through on this activity say about you?

____

____

MODULE 4

Interpersonal Effectiveness

Interpersonal Effectiveness: The Quick and Dirty

If I had to sum up interpersonal effectiveness in one sentence, it would be this: Interpersonal effectiveness is about getting what we need, protecting our self-respect, and maintaining relationships—without blowing things up or abandoning ourselves in the process.

Most people assume relationship problems happen because they are "bad communicators" or because other people are difficult, selfish, or emotionally unavailable. And sometimes that's true! But more often, the real issue is that people were never taught how to balance three competing needs at the same time:

1. What they want
2. The relationship
3. Their own self-respect

Interpersonal effectiveness skills exist because trying to juggle all three needs without any tools usually ends in resentment, withdrawal, emotional explosions, or quietly hating someone while still texting "no worries!" with a smiley face.

At its core, interpersonal effectiveness teaches us how to communicate clearly, assertively, and effectively while staying grounded in our values. It helps us ask for what we need without apologizing for just existing. It helps us say no without overexplaining or spiraling with guilt. It helps us set boundaries without turning into someone we don't recognize or someone we later feel ashamed of. And just as importantly, it helps us tolerate the reality that even when we communicate perfectly, the outcome is not guaranteed. It truly is the gift that keeps giving!

This module lives in DBT for a very specific reason. Many of the behaviors that bring people into therapy are not just about emotions—they're about relationships: explosive fights, chronic people-pleasing, fear of abandonment, avoidance of conflict, difficulty receiving feedback, and repeated patterns of feeling misunderstood, used, or unimportant. All that jazz. Without interpersonal effectiveness skills, relationships can become emotional landmines—and that constant relational stress feeds emotional dysregulation, impulsive behavior, shame, and burnout.

One of the hardest truths that clients (and clinicians!) wrestle with in this module is this: Being passive won't protect relationships, and being aggressive won't protect self-respect. Passive communication often leads to quiet resentment, scorekeeping, and emotional distance, all of which are massive drains on our well-being. On the other end, aggressive communication might get us short-term compliance, but it usually damages trust and connection between people. Interpersonal effectiveness skills help us find the middle path, which in this instance would be communication that is clear, direct, respectful, and most importantly, authentic.

I often tell clients to imagine relationships as a long road trip. If we never say that we are hungry, tired, or need to stop for a bathroom break, we might technically stay in the car together, but by hour six, we are furious, depleted, and secretly hoping the car breaks down. On the flip side, if we grab the wheel every time we are uncomfortable and start yelling directions, we might feel powerful in the moment, but eventually no one wants to be in the car with us because that can be dangerous. Interpersonal effectiveness involves learning how to speak up early, calmly, and clearly so the trip is sustainable, and who knows, maybe even fun!

Another important piece of this module is understanding that effectiveness is not the same thing as "niceness." When I use the word *effective*, I truly mean it in the most literal sense. DBT does not ask people to be agreeable, accommodating, or endlessly patient, because often, that isn't actually effective for getting our relational needs met. We are shooting for effective, which sometimes looks warm and collaborative. Other times it looks firm and boundaried. Sometimes it looks like accepting disappointment without self-abandonment. The goal here is not to control other people's responses (because that's not possible anyway), but to communicate in a way that aligns with our values and long-term goals.

Massive disclaimer for this module: Interpersonal effectiveness skills do not guarantee that people will respond well, change their behavior, or meet a client's needs. I know many clients go into this thinking that if they just communicate better or more clearly, the other person will respond with what they need. I hate to say it, but this is not always the case. Think of this as a yield sign on the on-ramp to the interpersonal effectiveness highway—it's a reminder for clients to slow down, check expectations, and focus on what is in *their* control. And although it doesn't guarantee any outcomes for clients, it does help them work on showing up clearly, honestly, and skillfully in their relationships. Over time, that builds self-respect, reduces resentment, and (ideally) creates healthier relational patterns. And if relationships do fall apart, as some inevitably will, they can walk away knowing they didn't lose themselves in the process. That's an interpersonal win in my book.

Interpersonal effectiveness is where DBT stops being just about coping and starts being about building a life worth living with other humans in it. And yes, that part is messy, vulnerable, and uncomfortable. But it is also where some of the most meaningful change happens!

To be clear: When I talk about discuss interpersonal effectiveness, I am addressing any and all kinds of relationships in someone's life—their friends, family, coworkers, partners, lovers, and acquaintances. Maybe even their favorite barista. My point is, these skills are meant to apply to all relationships, not just romantic ones.

Why Are Relationships So Hard Anyway?

Before I get into the nitty gritty of skills here, let's talk about why relationships can be so hard sometimes. Relationships can feel confusing, exhausting, or messy not because we are broken, needy, or doing something wrong. They're hard because they're the intersection of two or more nervous systems, histories, values, expectations, and communication styles, all trying to coexist in real time. That's a lot to manage even on a good day!

One of the biggest reasons relationships get complicated is because of differing values and goals. Two people can truly and genuinely care about each other and still want very different things. One person may value emotional closeness and frequent communication, while the other values independence and space. One person may prioritize stability and predictability, while the other values spontaneity and flexibility. Our values are never wrong—they're simply what we connect with. But when values and goals are misaligned or unspoken, conflict and resentment can creep in quietly—and then explode loudly later.

Another major factor is communication style. We all communicate based on what we learned growing up—not necessarily what works best in adulthood. Some people were taught to be direct and loud, and that's how they learned to get the job done. Others were taught to keep the peace at all costs. Some learned that expressing their needs could lead to punishment, dismissal, or conflict, so they learned to hint, tiptoe, or stay silent. Others learned that intensity was the only way to be heard. When these styles collide, misunderstandings are almost inevitable. One person thinks they're being clear, while the other hears criticism. One person thinks they are being respectful, while the other experiences distance or avoidance.

Expectations play a sneaky role too. Many expectations in relationships are unspoken, unconscious, and inherited from family systems, past relationships, or cultural norms. We expect people to know when we are upset. We expect partners to prioritize us in the same way we prioritize them. We expect friends to show up the way we would. The problem is that unmet expectations hurt just as much as broken promises, but the kick in the pants is that they are harder to address because they were never clearly stated in the first place! This is where resentment loves to set up camp.

As if all that wasn't enough, emotions make relationships even trickier. When we care about someone, the emotional stakes go way up. Fear of rejection, abandonment, conflict, or being seen as "too much" can hijack even the best intentions. In emotionally charged moments, our brains shift into threat mode, which makes listening harder, negative assumptions louder, and impulsive reactions much more likely. That's why we might say things we don't fully mean or struggle to say things we do mean when relationships feel tense. The nervous system is going haywire, which makes effective communication much more difficult.

Power dynamics matter too. Differences in age, finances, authority, emotional investment, or dependence can all influence how safe someone feels speaking up. If one person feels like they have more to lose, they may shrink themselves. If one person feels more secure or dominant, they may unintentionally dismiss or override the other. Truth be told, these dynamics are rarely malicious, but even still, they can quietly erode trust and self-respect over time if they are not acknowledged and properly addressed.

And finally, drumroll please . . . Relationships are messy because humans are messy! We bring our past wounds, attachment patterns, fears, and blind spots into every single connection we form. Old stuff can easily get activated in new situations, and a simple disagreement can suddenly feel like massive rejection. A boundary can feel like abandonment. A request can feel like criticism. None of this is necessarily bad or means the relationship is doomed—it just means we are human. And embracing the human messiness is part of the journey.

This is exactly why interpersonal effectiveness skills matter. It gives clients a shared language and a set of tools for navigating this wild complexity without defaulting to silence, aggression, or self-abandonment. These skills help them slow things down, clarify what they want, name what they feel, and communicate in ways that reduce damage rather than escalate it. I hate to say it, but many relationships will never be effortless. The good news is that with skill, they can become clearer, more honest, and a whole lot less painful.

The Six Core Interpersonal Effectiveness Skills

A practical overview of the skills that support healthy relationships

Before we jump into specific DBT interpersonal tools, like DEAR MAN, GIVE, and FAST, let's zoom out and look at the broader skill set that interpersonal effectiveness is built on. In DBT, we talk about six core interpersonal effectiveness skills that together determine how effectively someone navigates relationships. These are not personality traits or things that you're either born with or not. They are learnable, improvable skills. Most clients have strengths in some areas and gaps in others, and those gaps often explain the same relational patterns that keep showing up for them again and again.

Let's go through them one by one. I absolutely encourage you to go over these with your client as well to get a better sense of areas that need a bit more attention.

Skill 1: Knowing What You Want

This sounds ridiculously simple, but it's one of the most common breakdown points for a lot of folks. Many clients struggle here long before they ever open their mouths. They feel uncomfortable, resentful, or distressed in a relationship but can't clearly articulate what they want, need, or are aiming for. This is especially true for clients with a history of people-pleasing, trauma, or invalidation. If someone has learned that their needs don't matter or that expressing those needs creates conflict, they may stay vague, minimize, or convince themselves they "don't need anything."

Clinically, this shows up as indecision, chronic dissatisfaction, or the expectation that others should be mind readers. Without clarity here, even perfect communication skills won't land. This is where you can work with clients to clarify their wants and needs in relationships. This can range from small things, like wanting to talk things out calmly when both parties are upset, to big things, like wanting a big family that spends a lot of time together—and everything in between.

Skill 2: Asking for What You Want

Many clients believe they are bad at relationships, when in reality, they were just never taught how to ask directly and assertively. Asking for what you want seems simple on the surface, but it requires tolerating vulnerability, possible rejection, and discomfort, which is never easy. People tend to go one of a few ways with this: Some soften their requests until they disappear, overexplain to the point of confusion, or avoid asking for things altogether. Others swing to the opposite end, asking in ways that feel demanding or emotionally charged. And then there's the ever-popular passive-aggressive route where people don't ask at all but then act resentful and frustrated when their needs aren't met.

The skill of asking for what you want is about helping clients express their needs clearly, calmly, and respectfully, while also letting go of the fantasy that how they ask can control the outcome.

Skill 3: Negotiating Conflicting Wants

Many clients think conflict is a sign that a relationship is failing, when it can actually be a sign that two people have different needs, perspectives, or limits in that moment. Very normal, very human! People often struggle here because they believe someone has to "win" and someone has to "lose" (and not to be annoyingly DBT, but that's very black-and-white thinking). However, negotiation requires flexibility, validation, and a heavy dose of problem-solving. It also requires the practice of letting go of being "right" in favor of being effective.

Clinically, difficulty here shows up as rigid standoffs, emotional escalations, or giving in completely to avoid discomfort. Teaching this skill helps clients move away from all-or-nothing thinking and toward collaboration with their people.

Skill 4: Getting Information

This one is sneaky and often overlooked. Many interpersonal blowups happen not because of what was said, but because of assumptions we make about what was said—assumptions that were never checked. People often think they already know what the other person is thinking, feeling, or intending. Sometimes they might be right, but more often they are totally off base.

Now the question is, what makes it so hard for us to get information from people in our lives? Sometimes it's because we fear the answer, worry that we might be prying, or feel unsafe knowing the full truth. This skill teaches us (and our clients) how to gather information with curiosity rather than accusation. Don't get mad, get curious! Approaching conversations with curiosity tends to reduce misinterpretation and emotional reactivity in the other person. In session, this is often where we slow clients down and help them replace mind-reading assumptions with actual data.

Skill 5: Saying No and Setting Boundaries

This is the skill many clients desperately want but feel deeply conflicted about. Saying no seems so easy but can trigger immense guilt, fear of rejection, or shame, especially for clients who equate boundaries with being selfish or unkind. Other folks struggle with this because they set boundaries only after resentment has been built, leading to explosive or harsh delivery. This skill aims to help clients find the assertive middle ground, where boundaries are clear, calm, and consistent (the three C's). Clinically speaking, boundary work often reduces relationship burnout, resentment, and relationship instability more than almost any other intervention. This one is a gem for people-pleasers!

Skill 6: Acting According to Your Values

This is where interpersonal effectiveness intersects with self-respect. Clients may technically get what they want in a relationship, but at the cost of feeling small, dishonest, or misaligned with who they want to be. Maybe they agree to things they don't believe in just to keep the peace. Maybe they tolerate treatment that violates their standards because they're afraid of losing the relationship. Or maybe they say things they later regret because they were operating from anger rather than intention. In DBT, that doesn't fly anymore—not under my watch!

This skill asks clients to step back and consider not just what outcome they want, but what kind of person they want to be in that interaction. In other words, it invites them to ask themselves, "When I walk away from this conversation, how do I want to feel about the way I handled it?"

Values might include things like honesty, kindness, fairness, loyalty, accountability, integrity, or self-respect. Acting according to our values doesn't mean being perfect or always being on our moral high horse. It means trying to behave in ways that align with the principles that matter most to us, even when emotions are running high.

Clinically, difficulty with this skill often shows up as regret after interactions. Clients might say things like "I wish I hadn't said that," "I didn't handle that like myself," or "I just caved even though I didn't want to." These moments are often less about communication skills and more about losing connection with their values in the heat of the moment—or, as we would call it, self-abandonment.

Helping clients strengthen this skill involves slowing the interaction down and asking questions like "What kind of person do you want to be in this situation?" "What response would align with your values right now?" or "If you look back on this conversation tomorrow, what would you want to feel proud of?"

When clients begin acting in ways that align with their values, something important happens: Self-respect stays intact. And in DBT terms, protecting self-respect is one of the most stabilizing forces in relationships. Yay for self-advocacy!

Putting It All Together

As a clinician, this skills inventory gives you a powerful road map. Rather than framing relationship struggles as character flaws or attachment pathology, you can more easily identify which interpersonal skills need strengthening and tailor interventions in a more targeted way. This also helps clients feel less defective and more empowered. They are not bad at relationships. They are learning skills they were never taught!

And remember, this can take time and practice, just like any other skill. You wouldn't pick up a guitar for the first time and expect to rip "Stairway to Heaven." Same goes here: Clients don't learn how to set boundaries once and then become a boundaried king or queen. It takes time and practice.

As you move through this module, encourage clients to return to these six skills often. Progress here is not linear. Strengthening even one of these areas can create meaningful change across multiple relationships.

Client Worksheet

The Six Core Interpersonal Effectiveness Skills

A practical overview of the skills that support healthy relationships

Before we jump into specific interpersonal skills, let's take a snapshot of where you're starting. This is a gentle inventory that is simply meant to help you notice relationship patterns and identify which skills you may want to strengthen as you move through this module. There are no wrong answers. ☺

For each skill on this worksheet, rate yourself based on your typical relationship patterns, not your best or worst moments. This is your baseline, so to speak. Use a 0–10 scale, where 0 is "not skilled at all yet" and 10 is "I feel very confident in this area."

1. Knowing What You Want

This skill is about being able to identify what you want, need, or hope for in a relationship or situation. Sometimes people feel uncomfortable or upset in relationships but struggle to clearly name what exactly they want or need.

Right now, how skilled do you feel at knowing what you want in your relationships?

☐ 0 ☐ 1 ☐ 2 ☐ 3 ☐ 4 ☐ 5 ☐ 6 ☐ 7 ☐ 8 ☐ 9 ☐ 10

What makes it hard to identify your wants or needs?

____

____

2. Asking for What You Want

This skill is about clearly and directly expressing your needs or requests in a respectful way. Asking for what you want often requires vulnerability and the ability to tolerate discomfort, possible rejection, or conflict.

Right now, how skilled do you feel at asking for what you want?

☐ 0 ☐ 1 ☐ 2 ☐ 3 ☐ 4 ☐ 5 ☐ 6 ☐ 7 ☐ 8 ☐ 9 ☐ 10

What tends to get in your way when you try to ask for what you need?

____

____

3. Negotiating Conflicting Wants

This skill comes into play when your needs or preferences don't totally match someone else's. It requires flexibility, problem-solving, and letting go of the idea that someone has to "win" and someone has to "lose."

Right now, how skilled do you feel at negotiating disagreements or conflicts in your relationships?

☐ 0 ☐ 1 ☐ 2 ☐ 3 ☐ 4 ☐ 5 ☐ 6 ☐ 7 ☐ 8 ☐ 9 ☐ 10

What usually happens for you when there is disagreement?

____

____

4. Getting Information

This skill is all about checking your assumptions and gathering information instead of mind-reading or jumping to conclusions. Many conflicts happen not because of what was actually said, but because of assumptions we make about what was said.

Right now, how skilled do you feel at asking questions and getting clarification on things that might seem unclear in your relationships?

☐ 0 ☐ 1 ☐ 2 ☐ 3 ☐ 4 ☐ 5 ☐ 6 ☐ 7 ☐ 8 ☐ 9 ☐ 10

What makes it hard for you to ask for more information from others?

____

____

5. Saying No and Setting Boundaries

This skill is about protecting your time, energy, and emotional well-being by setting clear and respectful limits in your relationships. Many folks struggle here due to guilt, fear of disappointing others, worry about coming across as bossy or rude, or the tendency to wait until resentment builds before speaking up.

Right now, how skilled do you feel at saying no and setting boundaries in your relationships?

☐ 0 ☐ 1 ☐ 2 ☐ 3 ☐ 4 ☐ 5 ☐ 6 ☐ 7 ☐ 8 ☐ 9 ☐ 10

What emotions come up for you around setting boundaries?

____

____

6. Acting According to Your Values

This skill is about behaving in ways that align with the kind of person you want to be in relationships, even when emotions are intense and overwhelming. It focuses on self-respect and long-term alignment, not just getting a short-term outcome.

Right now, how skilled do you feel at acting according to your values in relationships?

☐ 0 ☐ 1 ☐ 2 ☐ 3 ☐ 4 ☐ 5 ☐ 6 ☐ 7 ☐ 8 ☐ 9 ☐ 10

In what situations is this hardest for you?

____

____

Reflection

Looking back at your ratings, what skill(s) do you want to focus on the most during this module?

____

____

What skill(s) do you already feel strong in?

____

____

As you move through the interpersonal effectiveness module, we'll keep returning to these six skills. Strengthening even one area can lead to meaningful changes across multiple relationships. Progress here is about practice, not perfection.

Assertiveness vs. Aggression

Finding the sweet spot between silence and explosions

This skill is all about helping clients understand that there is a meaningful difference between being assertive and being aggressive, even though many people have been taught to believe that they are one and the same. A lot of clients come into therapy with one of two core fears: "If I speak up, I'm being rude or selfish" or "The only way people listen to me is if I come in hot." Neither of these extremes tend to work very well long term.

Assertiveness is the middle path. It is clear, direct, respectful communication that honors both the client's needs and the relationship—simultaneously. Aggression, on the other hand, prioritizes getting a point across at the expense of the relationship, often through volume, threats, insults, blame, or just good ol' emotional intensity. Passivity does the opposite. It protects the relationship too much in the short term while quietly abandoning the self. Assertiveness asks clients to hold both at the same time. Dialectics, right?

The tricky part is that many folks confuse assertiveness with aggression because they have never seen assertiveness modeled in a healthy, and frankly correct, way. If they grew up in an environment where they got their needs met by yelling, control, guilt, or intimidation, then aggression may feel familiar and effective, even if it comes with consequences. On the other end, if they grew up learning that expressing their needs led to rejection, punishment, or emotional withdrawal, then they default to staying quiet until resentment boils over. Your job here is to normalize both patterns while gently coaching them toward something more sustainable—and more effective.

A helpful way to explain this to clients is to focus on intention and delivery. Aggression is about winning. Assertiveness is about communicating. Aggression sounds like "You never listen to me and I'm done asking." Assertiveness sounds like "I need you to hear me out because this matters to me." Same need. Very different impact.

When teaching this skill, I like to slow clients down and help them notice what their body is doing before they speak. Aggression often shows up when the sympathetic nervous system is already activated: raised voice, clenched jaw, rapid speech, rigid posture, high temperature. Assertiveness usually requires a bit of regulation first. Calm tone, steady pacing, and grounded body language are all key here. This is a great place to remind clients that assertiveness is not just a communication skill; it's also an emotion regulation skill.

When discussing assertiveness to people whose go-to is aggression, I often hear something like "But if I'm calm, they won't take me seriously" or "If I don't push hard, nothing changes." And to be honest, that's a real fear, especially for clients who have repeatedly felt dismissed or ignored. This fear makes sense given their lived experience; it's rarely about being aggressive just for fun. Rather than arguing with that belief, you can validate the fear and then do a little reality check. Aggression may get attention quickly, but it often damages trust, escalates conflict, or leads to regret. Assertiveness may feel slower or more vulnerable (and possibly less satisfying at first), but it increases the chances of being heard and actually getting their needs met without blowing up the relationship.

Another important teaching point is that assertiveness does not guarantee a yes. This is where clients get tripped up. They equate assertiveness with control over the outcome, like the stronger they go into this, the more likely it is that they will get their way. But in DBT, the goal is skillful self-respect, not outcome certainty. They can be perfectly assertive and still hear no. That does not mean they failed. It means they advocated for themselves in a way that aligned with their values. And that's where the work resonates.

In session, I often frame assertiveness as "clear, noticeable, and respectful." Clear means the other person does not have to guess what they want. Noticeable means they are not minimizing, apologizing, or burying the request. Respectful means no name-calling, no threats, and no emotional dumping disguised as honesty. This framing helps clients who worry they are either too much or not enough find a middle ground they can actually practice.

It can also be helpful to point out the emotional aftermath of ineffective communication. After aggression, people often report feelings of shame and regret, and the relationship itself can also suffer. When they think about a time they came in a little too hot, it's common that they felt guilt and shame afterward. After passivity, folks tend to report resentment, self-criticism, and emotional buildup. After assertiveness, even when the outcome is not someone hoped for, people often feel grounded, proud, or at least at peace with how they handled themselves. That emotional aftermath is an important data point worth highlighting!

You want to reinforce that assertiveness is a skill that improves with practice, not a personality trait that people either have or don't. I remind my clients all the time that these are skills, meaning they can be learned and built upon, just like a physical skill of learning to play the drums or painting. Clients do not need to become louder, tougher, or more confrontational. What more realistically helps is tools, language, and permission to take up space without burning it all down, as we can sometimes do (no judgment!).

Assertiveness vs. Aggression

Finding the sweet spot between silence and explosions

Many people believe that speaking up automatically means being rude, confrontational, or aggressive. Others believe that the only way to be heard is to raise their voice or push hard. In reality, there are three common communication styles:

1. **Passivity:** Protects the relationship but abandons your needs.
2. **Aggression:** Pushes your needs forward but damages the relationship. Aggression can show up either directly (through confrontation or force) or as **passive-aggression** (in which you express your needs indirectly through sarcasm, guilt, avoidance, or subtle digs rather than clear communication).
3. **Assertiveness:** The sweet spot that honors both your needs and the relationship at the same time.

Assertiveness is the proverbial middle path. It means expressing yourself clearly, respectfully, and honestly. Assertiveness does not guarantee the outcome you want, but it allows you to advocate for yourself while maintaining self-respect and protecting the relationship.

Let's explore what that looks like for you.

Step 1: Think of a Recent Interaction

Think about a recent situation where you felt frustrated, unheard, or upset with someone. Briefly describe the situation.

Who was involved?

____

____

What did you want or need in that moment?

____

____

Step 2: How Did You Respond?

In that situation, how did you respond?

☐ I stayed quiet or held my feelings in.
☐ I hinted at what I wanted but didn't say it clearly.
☐ I spoke up calmly and directly.
☐ I raised my voice or became intense.
☐ I criticized, blamed, or attacked.
☐ Something else: ______________

Looking back, do you think your response was mostly:

- ☐ Passive
- ☐ Assertive
- ☐ Aggressive
- ☐ Passive-aggressive
- ☐ A mix of these

Step 3: What Was Happening in Your Body?

Our bodies often give us clues about how we are communicating. Tune in to your body. Before or during the conversation, what did you notice in your body?

- ☐ Tight jaw
- ☐ Faster heartbeat
- ☐ Raised voice
- ☐ Rapid speech
- ☐ Feeling tense or hot
- ☐ Shutting down or going quiet
- ☐ Avoiding eye contact
- ☐ Other: ______________________________

What emotion was strongest for you in that moment?

____

____

Step 4: The Emotional Aftermath

After the interaction was over, how did you feel?

____

____

Sometimes the emotional aftermath gives us important information:

- After **aggression**, people often feel guilt, regret, or shame—and they may notice damage to the relationship.
- After **passive-aggression**, people often feel temporary satisfaction in the moment, followed by lingering tension, confusion in the relationship, or unresolved resentment because the real issue was never addressed directly.
- After **passivity**, people often feel resentment, frustration, or self-criticism.
- After **assertiveness**, people often feel proud, grounded, or at peace with how they handled themselves.

Which of these feels closest to your experience?

____

____

Step 5: Rewriting the Moment

Now imagine you could replay the conversation using assertiveness. Remember, assertiveness is:

- Clear: The other person understands what you want.
- Direct: You are not minimizing or apologizing for your needs.
- Respectful: No insults, threats, or blame.

Write what an assertive response might have sounded like.

Step 6: Practicing the Middle Ground

Think about the next time a similar situation might happen. What would help you respond more assertively? Identify one small thing you can try the next time you speak up.

DEAR MAN in Action

How to ask for what you need without blowing things up (or staying silent)

DEAR MAN is one of DBT's core interpersonal effectiveness skills. It's an acronym—go figure!—and it provides a structured, easy-to-follow framework for making requests and setting boundaries while maintaining self-respect in relationships. It is particularly useful for clients who struggle to speak up, feel chronically unheard, avoid conflict at all costs, become aggressive when emotions run high, or need support setting and maintaining boundaries. Personally speaking, I love to use it when I'm in conflict and want to express how I feel without getting caught up in Emotional Mind.

This skill is key because communication sits right at the center of every relationship, whether it's with a partner, friend, boss, family member, or colleague. Yet so many people struggle to ask for what they need in a way that actually works in their favor. Some clients avoid speaking up altogether—swallowing their needs and hoping the other person will just magically figure it out. Spoiler alert, they rarely do! Others communicate through anger, ultimatums, or emotional outbursts that may feel cathartic in the moment but often damage the relationship. Then there are the folks in the middle. These are the ones stuck in the exhausting middle ground of passive-aggressive comments, sarcasm, or hints, hoping someone will finally take the bait.

DEAR MAN exists because many clients were never taught how to ask for what they need without feeling guilty, selfish, too much, or afraid of conflict. In many parts of the world, and often depending on gender, culture, or social power, people are explicitly or implicitly taught that speaking up makes them difficult, dramatic, or selfish. Over time, those messages teach people to stay quiet, hint, or explode instead of asking directly. DEAR MAN offers a clear, step-by-step framework for assertive communication that is respectful, effective, and grounded. It also helps clients understand an important truth: that asking skillfully does not guarantee a yes, but it significantly increases the chances of being heard, taken seriously, and getting what they want.

In addition to fearing that they will come off as selfish, demanding, or "too much," many clients worry that making requests or setting boundaries will damage their relationships. That fear makes sense. Speaking up is scary, especially when it's new or when past experiences have taught them that it's unsafe to do so. What I make very clear to clients is this: While speaking up does carry discomfort, staying quiet is not free—meaning that their passivity comes with a cost, and that cost is often slow, creeping resentment. Unexpressed needs become the kindling for resentment, quietly building until they leak out through withdrawal, irritability, or emotional explosions. DEAR MAN helps clients get ahead of that cycle.

What Exactly Is DEAR MAN?

DEAR MAN is a framework for making requests or saying no in a way that is clear, respectful, and effective. It is a guide, not a script that clients have to memorize word-for-word. Let's walk through the letters in the acronym:

- **Describe** focuses on stating the facts neutrally and objectively using "I" statements. This means no opinions, no assumptions, and no loaded language. Just the observable facts. I like to throw in the suggestion of using the frame of "I've noticed" or "I've observed." For example, "I've noticed the sink has had dirty dishes in it every night this past week." Clean, objective, factual.
- **Express** is where we name how the situation affects us emotionally, using "I" statements again. "When the kitchen is messy, I feel overwhelmed and anxious."
- **Assert** is about clearly stating what we want or need to happen. This is where specificity really matters. Vague requests often lead to disappointment or unmet expectations. For anyone who's watched *Curb Your Enthusiasm*, don't get caught in an epic Larry versus Susie moment over something like "What is the call cut-off time for weeknights?" It's a hot mess, and you don't want it.

  While a request like "Can you do the dishes more?" might sound reasonable, it can mean different things to different people. To one person, "more" might mean daily, while to another it might mean every couple of days. A clearer version would be "Can we both make sure to wash our dishes and put them away by the end of each night?" When in doubt, encourage clients to be annoyingly clear to set themselves (and the relationship) up for success.
- **Reinforce** explains why meeting the request benefits both people. Everyone wants to know what's in it for them. This is human nature. This gives the other person a small amount of motivation to comply with the request. For example, "This would really help me feel less anxious, and I know you hate dealing with a pile of dishes at the end of the week, so doing them nightly would help with that too."
- **Mindfulness** means staying on topic and not getting pulled into side arguments or old grievances. We have *all* been in an argument that goes something like "Oh you are mad at me for X? What about the time when you Y!" If the other person brings up something unrelated, you want to coach clients to acknowledge it without abandoning the original request. Don't lose the plot, as they say. Stay on point. There's a rather easy way to do this and it sounds like "I hear that you have things you want to talk about too. Let's finish this dishes conversation first, and then we can come back to that because I want to hear your needs and wants too."
- **Appear confident** focuses on the delivery of the request. You want to encourage open body language, a steady tone, and eye contact, while minimizing apologizing or hedging language like "maybe" or "I don't know." Confidence here is about clarity, not aggression. Notice that

this part of the skill doesn't say "be confident"—it says "appear confident." You read that right! Fake it till you make it. Clients just need to appear like they feel strong here, even if they don't totally.

- **Negotiate** allows space for compromise and collaboration if needed. This might sound like "If dishes really aren't your thing, maybe I handle those and you take out the trash" or "What if we used paper plates on busy weeks?" Negotiation and compromise require problem-solving skills, so before clients present their request to the other person, help them come up with several compromises ahead of time!

Addressing Common Client Pitfalls

When clients try to practice DEAR MAN, it's normal for a variety of worries, habits, and "oops" moments to pop up. The good news is that many of these pitfalls are predictable and addressable:

- **Clients worry that being assertive will make them sound demanding.**
    - → Remind them that assertiveness is not about control or entitlement. It is about clarity and respect. You can ask for something while being kind at the same time. Dialectics!
- **Clients fear being told no.**
    - → This is where negotiation comes in, helping to prepare clients for flexibility before the conversation even happens. If they hear no, that doesn't necessarily mean it's the end of the road.
- **Clients worry about making the other person angry.**
    - → While we cannot control someone else's reaction, communicating calmly and directly increases the chances of a productive outcome and reduces regret later. If the other person does respond aggressively or unfavorably, here's where one of my favorite quotes can help: "We are not responsible for other people's emotions. We are only responsible for ourselves."
- **Clients avoid these conversations to prevent conflict.**
    - → In the short term, avoidance can feel easier, and sometimes it actually is. But in the long run, it usually fuels resentment and emotional distance, which slowly eats away at the relationship. Setting boundaries early on can prevent bigger conflicts later. Think early action, later benefit.
- **Clients treat DEAR MAN like a rigid script instead of a flexible skill.**
    - → When clients focus on saying it "perfectly," their delivery can sound a tad robotic or unnatural. Now it's totally okay to use DEAR MAN as a guide, but also encourage them to adapt the language so it fits their personality and feels authentic. When I do this in session, I will write down a script for them as we go using their language, not mine.

- **Clients expect immediate success and feel discouraged if the other person does not respond the way they hoped.**
    - → Reinforce that while DEAR MAN is fabulous at increasing effectiveness, it unfortunately cannot guarantee positive outcomes. You want clients to focus on the win—and the win is advocating for themselves skillfully, regardless of the outcome.
- **Clients worry about being accused of using "therapy talk."**
    - → This is too real, especially for clients who have loved ones who villainize therapy as a way to remain in unhealthy relationship patterns. I like to coach them to stay grounded and nondefensive. A simple response like "I'm just trying to be clearer about what I need" keeps the focus right where it belongs. Always remind them that learning new communication skills is leveling up, even if others do not immediately recognize or respond to it. Despite the outcome, they can be proud of their effort to work on their communication!

Client Worksheet

DEAR MAN in Action

How to ask for what you need without blowing things up (or staying silent)

Take a moment to pause and ground yourself. Asking for what you need can feel really vulnerable, especially if you're used to either staying quiet or speaking up only after emotions have built to a boiling point. If you notice your body feeling tense or your mind racing as you do this worksheet, that's completely normal. Take a slow breath, unclench your jaw or shoulders if they're tight, and remind yourself that this worksheet is just practice. We're just doing reps at the mental gym. You are not committing to having the conversation yet. You are simply organizing your thoughts so that if you do choose to speak up, you can do it in a way that is clear, respectful, and aligned with the kind of person you want to be in your relationships.

Before you create your DEAR MAN request, take a moment to notice your usual pattern in relationships. Do you tend to stay quiet and hope the situation resolves itself, or do things build until you explode? Just noticing this is already progress.

____

____

Step 1: What's the Situation?

Think about a real situation where you need to ask for something, set a boundary, or say no. This can be big or small. It can be with a partner, friend, family member, coworker, or anyone else in your life.

Briefly describe what's going on.

____

____

Step 2: Break It Down Using DEAR MAN

Now let's walk through each part of DEAR MAN. Remember, this is a framework, not a script. Use your own words. Nothing needs to sound perfect.

Describe

What are the observable facts of the situation? Stick to what can be seen or heard. No assumptions, no mind-reading.

"I've noticed that . . ."

____

____

***E*xpress**

How does this situation affect you emotionally? Use "I feel" statements.

"When this happens, I feel . . ."

***A*ssert**

What do you want or need to happen? Be specific and clear. Vague requests lead to vague results.

"What I'm asking for is . . ."

***R*einforce**

Why would meeting this request be helpful for both of you? What's the benefit on both sides?

"This would help me because . . ."

"This would also help you because . . ."

***M*indfulness**

If the conversation starts to drift or old issues get brought up, how will you stay on topic without escalating?

"If things go off track, I can say . . ."

***A*ppear Confident**

How do you want to show up physically and emotionally during this conversation? Think tone, posture, pacing, and eye contact.

"When I say this, I will try to . . ."

***N*egotiate**

If the other person can't meet your request exactly as stated, what compromises or alternatives would still work for you?

"Some options I'd be open to are . . ."

___

___

Step 3: Put It All Together

Now, write out your full DEAR MAN request as if you were saying it out loud. This does not need to be perfect. It just needs to be honest, clear, and respectful.

___

___

___

___

Step 4: Reality Check

Read what you wrote out loud, either in session or privately.

Does this sound like you?

☐ Yes ☐ No

Does anything feel unclear, overly apologetic, or overly harsh?

☐ Yes ☐ No

If so, what small tweaks would make it feel more natural?

___

___

Final Reflection

After you use this skill in real life, take a moment to reflect—not on whether you got the outcome you wanted, but on how you showed up for yourself.

Did you advocate for yourself clearly?

☐ Yes ☐ No

Did you stay grounded rather than reactive?

☐ Yes ☐ No

Did you act in a way that aligns with your values?

☐ Yes ☐ No

Even if the answer you received wasn't what you hoped for, using DEAR MAN is still a win. Speaking up skillfully is a form of self-respect, and that counts regardless of how the other person responds. Give yourself the kudos you deserve in doing something hard here!

GIVE FAST

Protect the relationship. Protect yourself.

Now that you better understand DEAR MAN, an important next step is to help clients recognize that *what* they ask for and *how* they show up while asking are two different skills. DEAR MAN focuses on effectiveness. GIVE and FAST focus on relationship care and self-respect. All three are meant to work together, like a well-coordinated group project where everyone actually does their part. Here's a helpful way to explain this to clients:

DEAR MAN helps you clearly say what you need.
GIVE helps you protect the relationship while you say it.
FAST helps you protect your self-respect, no matter the outcome.

GIVE: Keeping the Relationship Intact

Clinically, GIVE is often the antidote for clients who communicate accurately but harshly. They may technically "say it right" yet still damage the relationship through their tone or delivery. GIVE helps them balance that! It is especially useful for clients who care deeply about maintaining connection or who fear that being direct will damage the relationship. These skills help soften delivery without watering down the message. Let's walk through the letters in the acronym:

- **Gentle** encourages clients to avoid attacks, threats, or sarcasm. Being gentle does not mean being passive. It means speaking in a way that is calm, respectful, and non-escalating. For example, instead of saying, "You never help and I'm sick of doing everything myself," a gentle version might sound like "I'm feeling overwhelmed, and I'd like to talk about how we can split things more evenly."
- **Interested** reminds clients to listen and show curiosity about the other person's experience. This helps reduce defensiveness and increases the likelihood of collaboration. For example, after making a request, a client might say, "What do you think?" or "I want to understand what feels hard about this for you." Even nodding, maintaining eye contact, or reflecting back what the other person said counts here.
- **Validate** means acknowledging the other person's feelings or perspective, even if they disagree. Validation does not equal agreement. It simply communicates, "I see you." For example, "I can see why you'd feel frustrated coming home tired" or "It makes sense that this feels stressful for you given everything on your plate."
- **Easy manner** involves using warmth and humor when appropriate and maintaining relaxed body language. This can be especially helpful for clients who come across as rigid or intense when anxious. For example, a client might smile gently and say, "I promise I'm not trying to start World War III over the dishes" before continuing with their request. Or they might intentionally slow their speech and take a breath before responding.

FAST: Protecting Self-Respect

While GIVE focuses on the relationship, FAST ensures the client does not lose themselves in the process. FAST is a game changer for people-pleasers, who chronically abandon themselves in order to keep the peace. Without this skill, they may say yes when they want to say no, overapologize, or compromise their values—all in an attempt to avoid conflict. With FAST, they learn to reframe assertiveness as an act of self-respect rather than selfishness. Here's what the acronym means:

- **Fair** is about the client being fair to both themselves and the other person. This helps clients move away from extremes of self-blame or entitlement. For example, instead of thinking, "Their needs matter more than mine" or "I'm right and they're wrong," a fair stance might sound like "Both of our needs matter here, and I want to find a solution that respects both of us."
- **Apologies (limited)** reminds clients not to overapologize for having needs, feelings, or boundaries. Excessive apologizing erodes self-respect and weakens the message they are trying to communicate. For example, "I'm sorry for snapping at you earlier" is appropriate because it acknowledges the behavior that caused harm. In contrast, saying "I'm sorry for needing reassurance" or "I'm sorry for bringing this up" makes legitimate needs seem "wrong," which erodes self-respect.
- **Stick to values** encourages clients to act in alignment with what matters to them, even when it's uncomfortable. This is especially important when the outcome is uncertain. For example, consider a client who values honesty and reliability but feels pressured to yes to something they know they cannot follow through on. While giving in to the request may temporarily keep the peace, it violates their values and damages self-trust. Sticking to their values in this situation might sound like "I really want to help, but I can't commit to that right now."
- **Truthful** means not exaggerating, manipulating, or minimizing the situation. Honesty builds both internal integrity and external trust. For example, instead of saying, "You always ignore me," a more truthful statement would be "I felt ignored when I didn't hear back from you yesterday." Instead of pretending something is fine when it isn't, truthfulness sounds like "I'm not okay with this, *and* I want to talk about it."

How to Teach the Integration

When teaching DEAR MAN alongside GIVE and FAST, it can help to explain that not every situation requires all three skills at full intensity. Some conversations might call for more GIVE, others more FAST. The goal is balance. A simple way to frame it for clients is as follows: Use DEAR MAN to structure your request. Layer on GIVE to protect the relationship. Anchor it with FAST to protect your self-respect.

Client Worksheet

GIVE FAST

Protect the relationship. Protect yourself.

Difficult conversations can feel overwhelming, especially when you're trying to be honest about your needs while keeping the relationship intact. This worksheet is designed to help you slow things down and approach the conversation in a way that protects both the relationship and your self-respect. Remember, communication is not just about *what* you say, but also about *how* you say it and how you show up while saying it. Here's a simple way to think about the interpersonal effectiveness skills you've learned:

- DEAR MAN helps you clearly say what you need.
- GIVE helps you protect the relationship while you say it.
- FAST helps you protect your self-respect, no matter the outcome.

Together, these skills help you communicate in a way that is effective, respectful, and aligned with your values. Let's walk through the GIVE and FAST skills step by step.

Step 1: Think About the Conversation

Think of a situation where you want to ask for something, set a boundary, or address a problem with someone. Briefly describe the situation.

Who is involved?

____

____

What do you hope will happen after the conversation?

____

____

Step 2: GIVE (Protecting the Relationship)

The GIVE communication skills help you keep the relationship safe and reduce defensiveness.

Gentle

How can you say what you need in a calm and respectful way (no attacking, blaming, or sarcasm)?

"I can convey my message gently by saying . . ."

____

____

Interested

How can you show curiosity and openness to the other person's perspective?

"I can show interest by saying . . ."

Validate

What might be understandable about the other person's feelings or perspective?

"I can validate their experience by saying . . ."

Easy Manner

How can you keep your tone, body language, and energy relaxed during this conversation?

"I can keep an easy manner by . . ."

Step 3: FAST (Protecting Your Self-Respect)

The FAST skills help you stay true to yourself and your values during the conversation, even if it is uncomfortable or doesn't go the way you'd hoped.

Fair

How can you be fair to both yourself *and* the other person in this situation—rather than putting yourself last or assuming you are completely right?

"I can be fair to both of us by . . ."

Apologies

While it's important to apologize for any harm you've caused, you want to avoid overapologizing for having needs, setting boundaries, or bringing up something uncomfortable. Identify what you do *not* need to apologize for.

"I might feel tempted to apologize for . . ."

"But I don't need to apologize for this because . . ."

Stick to Values

What values do you want to honor in this conversation? (Examples: honesty, kindness, respect, fairness, responsibility)

"My values in this situation are . . ."

"I can act in alignment with those values by . . ."

Truthful

How can you communicate honestly about what's happening without exaggerating or minimizing the situation?

"A truthful statement I could use is . . ."

Step 4: Bringing It All Together

Imagine having this conversation while using the GIVE and FAST skills. How would you want to show up in that moment?

What reminder might help you stay grounded during the conversation?

Final Reflection

Remember, using these skills does not guarantee the outcome that you want. The goal is *not* to control the other person's response—it's to communicate in a way that protects both the relationship and your self-respect. Either way, showing up skillfully is still a win!

After the conversation, reflect on these questions:

Did you communicate respectfully?

☐ Yes ☐ No

Did you stay true to your values?

☐ Yes ☐ No

Did you advocate for yourself clearly?

☐ Yes ☐ No

The Emotional Bank Account

How relationships are built, damaged, and repaired over time

Clients often come into therapy confused about why they feel so reactive, guarded, or resentful toward certain people, even when the current issue seems minor. You might hear things like "I don't know why this bothered me so much" or "If anyone else had said that I wouldn't care." Folks, I give you: the Emotional Bank Account (or EBA for short)—a handy tool that explains this disconnect.

The objective of the EBA is to help clients understand how everyday interactions impact relationship safety, trust, and emotional closeness over time. It gives them a concrete way to understand why some relationships feel easier, safer, or more forgiving while others feel tense, fragile, or exhausting, even when the current conflict seems "small."

The EBA is a concept developed by John Gottman that explains relationships through the metaphor of deposits and withdrawals. Every interaction we have with someone either adds to our emotional balance or subtracts from it. Over time, this balance determines how resilient the relationship is, especially during conflict or stress.

At this point, you might be thinking, "If this is a Gottman skill, why is it in a DBT book?" Honestly speaking? Because it's too good to leave out! This model fits beautifully within DBT's interpersonal effectiveness framework because it reinforces a core DBT principle: that getting our needs met while protecting both ourselves and the relationship requires long-term thinking, not just momentary relief.

This framework also gives clients language for understanding relational dynamics without pathologizing themselves or others. Instead of "You raised your voice and you're an asshole," clients learn to say, "When you raised your voice, it was a big withdrawal for me." That shift supports accountability, boundary-setting, and compassion all at the same time. And that balance is very DBT.

The EBA also naturally pairs with DEAR MAN, GIVE, and FAST. A client with a fuller emotional account will have an easier time making requests, negotiating boundaries, and tolerating disappointment. Conversely, when the account is depleted, even skillful communication may feel harder and less effective.

This model is especially helpful for clients who struggle with emotional sensitivity, rejection sensitivity, or black-and-white thinking in relationships. It shifts the conversation away from "Who's right?" and toward "What has been happening in this relationship over time?"

Introducing the Metaphor

Explain that every relationship has an emotional bank account. Positive interactions—being kind, going out of your way, a smile, a good luck text, acknowledging someone's effort—are deposits. Hurtful, neglectful, or invalidating interactions are withdrawals. No relationship avoids withdrawals entirely. What matters is the overall balance!

When an EBA is full, relationships have cushion. There is goodwill, trust, and emotional safety. Small mistakes or miscommunications are easier to tolerate, repair happens more naturally, and conflict feels less threatening. Think about it like a real bank account: Taking out $100 from a $5,000 account is going to feel a lot safer than taking out $100 from a $500 account. When the account is low or overdrawn, even the smallest interactions can feel loaded. We are quicker to assume bad intent, we are more emotionally reactive, and we are less willing to give the benefit of the doubt.

A key teaching point is that intent does not determine whether something functions as a deposit or a withdrawal. *Impact does.* A comment meant as a joke can still land as a withdrawal if it causes harm, because the receiver's experience is what matters. Similarly, forgetting a commitment, even when it is unintentional, still costs the relationship something.

This is often a lightbulb moment for clients, especially those who rely heavily on cognitive empathy (a.k.a. the tendency to think through other people's feelings more than feel them). They may fully understand why something happened and still find themselves unable to let it go. That is not stubbornness or immaturity. It's lingering emotional pain from the interaction that hasn't been repaired yet. Naming this distinction helps clients understand that insight alone does not heal relational wounds. Repair does.

It is also important to emphasize that deposits are often small and consistent, not grand gestures. Many clients believe they need to "fix" relationships with big conversations or dramatic apologies while overlooking the daily behaviors that actually build trust. Think of it like that big jug at the front of the house that perhaps you throw pocket change into when you get home. A quarter here, a dime there. Nothing major, but at the end of the year, maybe you take it to the grocery store to exchange it for cash and get $300. They can seem like small, nothing-like gestures, yet because they are easy to make and consistent, they add up.

Deposits, Withdrawals, and Skillful Repair

The accompanying client-facing worksheet outlines Gottman's six ways of making deposits:

1. Showing interest
2. Keeping commitments
3. Clarifying expectations
4. Attending to small moments
5. Operating with integrity
6. Apologizing after harm

One of the most DBT-consistent pieces of this model is the idea that apologizing after a withdrawal *is itself a deposit*. Clients often believe that once damage is done, it is permanent. Teaching repair as an active, skillful process helps counter hopelessness and supports accountability without shame.

It is also important to acknowledge that even the strongest relationships can go bankrupt if there are repeated withdrawals without repair. No amount of history or love can compensate for an account that is consistently overdrawn. This is where boundaries become essential. Some clients use the EBA concept to justify staying in relationships where they are constantly making deposits while the other person keeps withdrawing. That is not a relationship running on low funds. That is a relationship operating in the red. Helping clients recognize the difference between a temporarily depleted account and one that is chronically empty is a crucial clinical intervention. At some point, the work shifts from "How do I invest more?" to "Is this account even safe to keep open?"

When teaching this skill, reinforce that the goal is not perfection. Everyone makes withdrawals—that's totally normal and very human. The goal is awareness, repair, and *intentional* investment. Clients do not need to keep score, but they do need to notice patterns.

Client Worksheet

The Emotional Bank Account

How relationships are built, damaged, and repaired over time

Every relationship in life comes with its own emotional bank account (or EBA). And most of us are managing several of these accounts at once, each shaped by its own history, patterns, and repeated interactions over time. This worksheet is about bringing some awareness to where those accounts currently stand—what deposits have been made and what withdrawals have accumulated. There are no "right" or "wrong" answers here. You're simply getting curious about where things stand right now for you and your people!

Step 1: Your Relationships

Think about the key relationships in your life. These might include romantic partners, close friends, family members, coworkers, or anyone who has emotional weight for you. In the following space, list one or more significant relationships in your life.

____

____

____

____

Step 2: Assign an Emotional Balance

Now you're going to estimate the current balance of each emotional bank account. To keep this simple, use the following scale:

+100 = Very full account: high trust, warmth, and goodwill
0 = Neutral: neither especially close nor especially tense
–100 = Deeply overdrawn: high tension, resentment, or emotional strain

For the first relationship you listed, assign a number that feels accurate to you right now.

Relationship: ______________________________

Current Balance (between –100 and +100): ______________________________

Why do you think this account sits here right now? Consider both your deposits and withdrawals and the other person's.

____

____

Use a separate piece of paper to repeat this step for each relationship you listed in step 1. As you do this, notice what comes up emotionally. Relief, sadness, clarity, defensiveness, grief—all of it is allowed. Awareness is the goal here.

Step 3: Noticing Patterns

Take a moment to reflect on what you're seeing across your EBAs.

Are there relationships where you are consistently making deposits but frequent withdrawals keep draining the balance?

____

____

Are there relationships that feel well-funded, meaning that even when a withdrawal (a.k.a. conflict) happens, it feels safer or more forgiving?

____

____

Are there relationships where the balance has shifted over time, either growing steadily or slowly getting drained?

____

____

Step 4: Where Do You Want to Invest?

Now choose one or two relationships you genuinely want to invest in right now.

Relationship you want to invest in: ______________________ Current balance: __________

Relationship you want to invest in: ______________________ Current balance: __________

For each of these relationships, you're going to look at how to make intentional deposits.

Step 5: Making Deposits on Purpose

The following list includes the six ways to make deposits into an EBA. As you read through them, think specifically about how each one could show up in the relationship(s) you chose. You do not need to do all of these. Small, consistent deposits matter more than grand gestures.

1. **Showing interest and paying attention**

   How could you show more genuine interest in this person's thoughts, feelings, or experiences?

   ____

   ____

2. **Keeping commitments**
   Are there promises, big or small, that matter in this relationship? Is there anything you said you'd do that needs follow-through?

   ____

   ____

3. **Clarifying expectations**
   Are there any unspoken assumptions in this relationship that might need to be clarified? What is your love language? What is theirs? What kinds of "deposits" carry the most weight for them?

   ____

   ____

4. **Attending to the little things**
   What are one or two small, thoughtful actions you could take this week that could build goodwill?

   ____

   ____

5. **Showing personal integrity**
   How can you show up in a way that aligns with your values and also respects theirs?

   ____

   ____

6. **Apologizing when a withdrawal has been made**
   Has there been a recent withdrawal that needs acknowledgment, accountability, or repair?

   ____

   ____

Remember, emotional bank accounts are built over time. No single conversation or gesture determines the balance. What matters here is the pattern. And don't forget, you are not responsible for funding every relationship on your own. Awareness helps you decide where to invest, where repair is possible, and where boundaries may be needed. Healthy relationships require contributions from both sides. This is a shared account, not a solo GoFundMe!

Understanding Boundaries

Understanding your personal limits in relationships

Boundaries might be a foundational interpersonal skill, but it's one that many clients were never explicitly taught. So many folks come into therapy with a vague sense that "Yeah, I know boundaries matter . . ." yet they struggle to define what a boundary actually *is*. Because of that, I like to start by defining it: A boundary is what someone is and is not comfortable with in a relationship. It is not a punishment, a threat, or a demand for someone else to change. It is information about you!

So what's the point in learning how to set boundaries? It's actually pretty simple. When boundaries are unclear or unspoken, people tend to default to people-pleasing, avoidance, or emotional blowups. Boundary work offers a cleaner and more sustainable alternative: It supports our mental health while also preserving relationships that matter to us.

In my experience, many clients associate boundaries with conflict, rejection, or being "too much." We're going to pull an UNO reverse here and dispel that myth. Instead of seeing boundaries as "too much," we can reframe them as a way to reduce resentment and emotional exhaustion in relationships. And what is resentment, if not relationship cancer? When clients can start to look beyond the initial discomfort of setting a boundary, it becomes clearer that they actually aren't doing themselves (or their relationships) any favors by staying quiet.

Types of Boundaries

Like anything else, it can help to break boundaries into smaller categories to make them more digestible and to help clients see where their limits actually lie. At the same time, it's important to remember that boundaries are never one-size-fits-all, meaning that some clients may be very skilled at setting physical or time boundaries but struggle with emotional boundaries. They might say, "I have no problem setting boundaries at work or with friends, but when it comes to my parents, I just can't say no!" Naming these specific boundary experiences gives clients the language to describe experiences they've felt but couldn't put into words.

Here are the types of boundaries you'll want to explore with clients:

- **Intellectual boundaries** relate to how we share and discuss our thoughts, opinions, beliefs, and values with others. Some people love a good debate, while others don't enjoy having their beliefs constantly challenged. These boundaries help us decide how much we want to engage with unsolicited advice, heated discussions, or controversial topics. Healthy intellectual boundaries remind us that it's okay to respectfully disagree without feeling like we have to defend our beliefs all the time. Think: "No, Uncle Pete, I do not want to discuss politics at the dinner table."

- **Physical boundaries** involve our comfort around personal space and touch—basically, our personal bubble. Think hugs, high-fives, physical affection, or how close someone stands to us. Physical boundaries also cover privacy around our bodies, health, and personal routines.
- **Emotional boundaries** determine how much of our inner world we share, when we share it, and with whom. They also help us decide how much emotional weight we're willing to carry for others. Healthy emotional boundaries allow us to care deeply about people without feeling responsible for fixing or managing their emotions. Think: "Not my monkeys, not my circus."
- **Sexual boundaries** relate to our comfort around sexual topics, jokes, behaviors, and physical intimacy. These include preferences around pacing, consent, communication, and how sexual content is shared or discussed. These boundaries are deeply personal and can look very different depending on the relationship. There is no right or wrong here.
- **Time boundaries** help us manage our availability, energy, and commitments. This includes how quickly we respond to messages, how much we say yes to, how we balance our responsibilities with downtime, and how much we have in our social battery. When time boundaries get blurry, people often find themselves overcommitted, exhausted, or quietly resentful. Boundaries can help us avoid that!
- **Material boundaries** pertain to our "stuff"—our belongings, money, property, and other resources. These boundaries guide our decisions about lending items, sharing finances, or borrowing money. Things can get tricky pretty fast when our material boundaries aren't clearly communicated. We've all been in that uncomfortable "Are you going to pay me back?" situation.
- **Digital boundaries** relate to our online lives and devices, setting expectations around texting, social media, location sharing, email, and overall digital privacy. In today's world, digital boundaries matter more than ever, even though many people forget to set them. One of my favorite ways to help clients with this? "After 5 p.m., I will not be responding to emails." Ugh. GOLD.
- **Energy boundaries** govern how much emotional, mental, and physical energy we give to others. This includes how much we listen to venting, how much we take on other people's problems, and how often we step into caretaker mode. When energy boundaries are weak, we often feel drained and can't quite figure out why. Think the infamous energy vampire, Collin Robinson.
- **Role boundaries** clarify what is actually our responsibility in a relationship—and what isn't. Without this type of boundary, we can slip into roles we never signed up for, like the mediator, rescuer, parent, or unofficial therapist in the relationship. Unfortunately, this shows up a lot in families and caregiving dynamics.
- **Values boundaries** keep us aligned with the kind of person we want to be. These boundaries come into play when we feel pressured to go along with something that doesn't sit right

with our beliefs, ethics, or long-term goals. Holding our values boundaries means choosing integrity, even when it's uncomfortable or we feel pressured.

When working with clients who want to focus on boundaries, it can be helpful to treat this list as a collaborative exploration rather than a checklist to complete. I encourage you to move slowly through each boundary type and to invite clients to identify as many specific, personal boundaries as they can within each category. This might sound like "What are you comfortable with here?" and just as importantly, "What are you *not* comfortable with?" The goal is not to decide what their boundaries should be, but to help them just notice preferences that exist, while validating that these preferences are okay. Many clients realize they have been violating their own boundaries long before anyone else ever did. This step aims to build awareness and clarity, which then makes later work on communicating and reinforcing boundaries way more effective.

Quality of Boundaries

Now that we've covered the different types of boundaries, let's zoom out and take a look at their quality and strength. We can break down boundaries into three categories—porous, rigid, and healthy—kind of like the three states of mind:

- **Porous boundaries** let too much in. People with porous boundaries may overshare personal information, say yes when they really want to say no, take on responsibilities that were never actually theirs, or feel responsible for managing other people's emotions. These folks are often incredibly kind, empathetic, and generous. The problem is that without enough boundaries, those strengths can quickly turn into exhaustion, resentment, and burnout. Yikes.
- **Rigid boundaries**, on the opposite side of the spectrum, keep too much out. Someone with rigid boundaries may appear distant, guarded, or emotionally shutdown. They may struggle with trust, keep people at arm's length, or avoid vulnerability altogether. Often, this style develops as a form of protection: If someone has been hurt, invalidated, or taken advantage of in the past, tightening those boundaries can feel like the safest option available. As a result, they put up walls to keep themselves safe.
- **Healthy boundaries** live in the middle. These allow people to stay open and connected to others while still protecting their own needs, limits, and values. Healthy boundaries let someone share without oversharing, say yes when they mean it (and no when they need to), and show up in relationships without abandoning themselves in the process. They allow for connection with discernment, flexibility without self-betrayal, and assertiveness without aggression.

Important note: Neither porous nor rigid boundaries are "bad." In fact, they often make sense when you consider a person's history. Porous boundaries may have developed in environments where connection depended on caretaking or self-sacrifice. Rigid boundaries may have formed in environments where vulnerability didn't feel safe. This normalizes something we see all the time in therapy: People often swing to one extreme or the other depending on their experiences, their fears, and what they've learned about relationships growing up. Rarely does someone naturally land in that balanced middle right away. Most of us have to learn our way there.

And just like most things we talk about in DBT, the goal is never perfection. The goal is simply awareness and adjustment. Boundaries aren't fixed traits. They are skills that can be strengthened, softened, and reshaped over time as clients learn what works for them and what doesn't. In my time, I have seen some clients go from extreme people-pleasers—exhausted and overextended in their lives—to "boundaried baddies" (yes, I made this term up) who protect themselves but also show up authentically for others. This is chef's kiss.

Client Worksheet

Understanding Boundaries

Understanding your personal limits in relationships

Boundaries often get a bad reputation. A lot of people think boundaries are about being mean, pushing people away, or creating conflict, when in reality, boundaries are much simpler than that. Simply put: A boundary is what you are and are not comfortable with in a relationship.

Without boundaries in your relationships, you run the risk of developing resentments, burnout, and emotional exhaustion. When your boundaries are unclear or unspoken, you tend to lean into people-pleasing, avoid difficult conversations, or eventually blow up when things feel like too much. But there is a solution! Getting clearer about your own boundaries gives you a healthier way to protect your energy while still maintaining relationships that matter to you.

This worksheet is meant to help you explore what your personal boundaries actually are. There are no right or wrong answers here—boundaries are just preferences, so any and all are allowed. As you read through each type of boundary, you might notice that you already have clear boundaries in some areas and very fuzzy ones in others. That's normal!

Intellectual Boundaries

These relate to how you share and discuss thoughts, opinions, beliefs, and values. This includes how comfortable you are with debating, receiving advice, being challenged, or talking about controversial topics.

Ask yourself: How do I feel when people challenge my opinions? Are there topics I prefer not to discuss, or only discuss with certain people?

What are your intellectual boundaries?

Physical Boundaries

These relate to personal space, touch, privacy, and your body. This includes comfort with hugging, physical affection, sharing space, and privacy around your body or health.

Ask yourself: What kinds of touch feel okay to me, and what doesn't? How much physical space or privacy do I need?

What are your physical boundaries?

____

____

____

____

Emotional Boundaries

These relate to how much emotional information you share, when you share it, and with whom. This includes limits around venting, emotional caretaking, and taking on other people's feelings.

Ask yourself: Do I feel responsible for managing other people's emotions? Who do I feel safe being emotionally open with?

What are your emotional boundaries?

____

____

____

____

Sexual Boundaries

These involve comfort around sexual topics, jokes, physical intimacy, pacing, consent, and communication about sex. These boundaries can look very different depending on the relationship.

Ask yourself: What feels okay for me sexually right now? What feels uncomfortable or too fast?

What are your sexual boundaries?

____

____

____

____

Time Boundaries

These relate to how you manage your availability, schedule, and energy. This includes responsiveness, work-life balance, and how much time you give to others versus yourself.

Ask yourself: Do I often feel overcommitted or stretched thin? What does a reasonable amount of time and access look like for me?

What are your time boundaries?

Material Boundaries

These involve your boundaries with money, belongings, property, and resources. This includes your preferences regarding lending items, sharing finances, and expectations around ownership.

Ask yourself: How do I feel about lending money or belongings? Have I ever felt resentful because expectations weren't clear?

What are your material boundaries?

Digital Boundaries

These relate to the limits you set regarding phones, texting, social media, email, and online access. This includes response times, location sharing, privacy, and online presence.

Ask yourself: Do I feel pressured to always be available digitally? What level of access feels healthy for me?

What are your digital boundaries?

Energy Boundaries

These involve how much emotional, mental, or physical energy you give to others, including caretaking, problem-solving, listening, and crisis support.

Ask yourself: Do I often feel drained after interacting with certain people? How much energy do I realistically have to give?

What are your energy boundaries?

Role Boundaries

These relate to clarity around what is and is not your role in a relationship. This includes not taking on roles like rescuer, therapist, parent, or mediator.

Ask yourself: Do I take responsibility for things that aren't actually mine to fix? What roles do I tend to slip into automatically?

What are your role boundaries?

Values Boundaries

These involve the limits you set to stay aligned with your core values, even when there is pressure to please others, avoid conflict, or fit in.

Ask yourself: Are there situations where I go against my values to keep the peace? What matters most to me long term?

What are your values boundaries?

Noticing the Quality of Your Boundaries

Once you've identified the types of boundaries that matter most to you, the next step is to notice how strong or flexible those boundaries are. The goal is not to create perfect boundaries. That's not a real thing. The goal is to have flexible boundaries that can change depending on the situation and the relationship, while still protecting you.

- **Porous boundaries:** These often show up as oversharing, difficulty saying no, overgiving, or feeling responsible for other people's emotions.

- **Rigid boundaries:** These can look like emotional distance, shutting down, avoiding vulnerability, or keeping people at arm's length to feel safe.
- **Healthy boundaries:** These sit in the middle. They allow connection while still protecting your needs, energy, and self-respect.

Do your boundaries tend to be more porous, rigid, or somewhere in between?

___

___

___

Which boundary types feel strongest for you right now?

___

___

___

Which ones feel hardest to maintain?

___

___

___

Just noticing these patterns is a powerful first step. From here, you can work on how to communicate and reinforce these boundaries in a way that feels safe, effective, and aligned with who you are. Good work!

Saying No with Confidence

Because saying no doesn't make you selfish

Saying no is a core part of healthy boundaries and healthy relationships. It might not seem like a big deal to not learn this skill, but truth be told, without the ability to say no, relationships can start to feel one-sided and exhausting on a good day . . . and unsafe and overwhelming on a bad one. It's a bit like driving a car with a gas pedal but no brakes. Clients might keep moving forward, but they don't actually have any real control or safety.

When clients learn to say no, they are not learning how to be rude or selfish. They are learning how to advocate for themselves honestly. This distinction is critical to emphasize early, especially for clients who equate self-advocacy with guilt, rejection, or abandonment.

Before teaching the mechanics of how to say no, let's explore why so many people have a hard time with this in the first place. Here are some reasons I have found to be true for many folks:

- **Fear of disappointing others:** People fear that saying no will let others down or damage their relationships.
- **Desire to be liked:** Some people worry that saying no will make them seem unhelpful or unlikeable. Identity can play into this as well: "Who am I if I'm not being helpful?"
- **Difficulty setting boundaries:** People may struggle to establish and maintain boundaries, making it hard to say no even when they want to.
- **Fear of conflict:** Some people worry that saying no will lead to arguments or negative consequences, so they avoid it altogether.
- **Low self-esteem:** People with low self-esteem may have trouble valuing their own needs and opinions, making it hard to assert themselves and say no. Almost like thinking, "My needs don't matter."
- **Social expectations:** In some cultures or social situations, saying no may be seen as impolite or unacceptable, leading people to say yes even when they don't want to.
- **Lack of assertiveness skills:** People may not know how to communicate their needs and boundaries effectively, making it challenging to say no.

How to Say No

It's important to start off by saying there isn't just one "right" way to say no. Different situations call for different approaches, obviously! Encourage clients to read the room, be aware of context, and know their audience. The following are several options. Clients can choose the one(s) that feels most realistic for them in the moment.

Appear Confident

Notice that I didn't say *be* confident. I said *appear* confident. (You might recall that's the second A in DEAR MAN!) Perceived confidence matters more than the exact words. Standing or sitting upright, making eye contact, and using a steady tone (as best we can) can help the message land clearly. When a client's delivery is confident, people are less likely to push back.

Be a Broken Record

If someone keeps pushing after a client has already said no, they can calmly repeat their response without arguing or explaining further. Keep it short and consistent. They are not required to defend their boundary. For example:

FRIEND: "Can you come out tonight? It'll be fun. You can just stay for a little."

CLIENT: "Thanks for inviting me, but I'm not able to hang out tonight."

FRIEND: "Oh come on, you've been so busy lately. You deserve it!"

CLIENT: "I hear you, but unfortunately I'm still not going to be able to make it."

FRIEND: "Seriously? Just one drink?"

CLIENT: "I know, I'm bummed too, but my answer is still no. Thank you for the invite!"

Use a Polite, Brief Response

Sometimes saying, "No, thank you" is enough. Clients don't owe anyone more information than they want to give. They don't need a long explanation or the perfect wording. Often, simple and clear is best. For example:

- "I'm sorry, that doesn't work for me right now."
- "I'm not comfortable with that."
- "That's not going to work for me, but I appreciate you asking."
- "I need to set a boundary here, so I'm going to say no."

The words themselves are simple. The hard part is giving themselves permission to say them.

Use Light Humor

In low-stakes situations, humor can help break tension while still holding the boundary. This works best when safety and power dynamics are not a concern. Here are some examples:

- "Yikes, sorry babe—can't swing it!"
- "Can't help ya, kid." (in a lighthearted tone)
- Phoebe from *Friends* when she says, "Oh I wish I could, but I don't want to."
- Roger from *American Dad* when he sings, "Noooooo!"

Make an Excuse

If saying no directly feels too hard right now, it's okay for clients to use a small, harmless excuse. They are still honoring our boundary, even if they're not ready to explain it fully. For example:

- "I have to get up early."
- "I have other plans."
- "I'm not feeling well."

Give a Reason

When clients feel more comfortable, they can offer a truthful reason. This is different from overexplaining. One honest sentence is enough. For example:

FRIEND: "Hey! Can you cover my shift for work tonight?"

CLIENT: "Thanks for asking, but I need to prioritize my own self-care, so I can't take on any additional responsibilities right now."

FRIEND: "I'm going up to the bar, what are you drinking tonight?"

CLIENT: "I'm actually not drinking at the moment; I'm in recovery."

Offer an Alternative

Sometimes no doesn't mean "never" or "not at all." Clients can say no while still offering a different option that does feel okay for them. For example:

FRIEND: "Hey, can you attend the work event I'm throwing next week?"

CLIENT: "No, I'm sorry; I can't attend the event, but I can help you brainstorm some ideas!"

FRIEND: "Would you be able to lend me some money?"

CLIENT: "I'm not comfortable lending money out, but if it helps, I'm pretty good with finances and am happy to help you do a budget if you'd like."

Use an Assertive Delay

Clients are allowed to pause before answering. Taking time to think is a boundary. They do not have to decide on the spot. This can be as simple as "Let me check my schedule and get back to you" or "I need to think about this, and I'll let you know later." For example:

POTENTIAL BOSS: "We love you! You got the job! Will you be coming on board with our team?"

CLIENT: "Thank you so much for the offer. I'm going to need to take some time to sift through this offer. I'd love to get back to you by early next week."

Confront the Behavior

If someone repeatedly ignores a client's boundaries, it may be necessary to address the situation directly. Naming the pattern can be a powerful way to protect themselves. For example:

> PERSON: "So what's up, are we going to hook up or not?"
>
> CLIENT: "Hey, so you've made several advances, and I've already told you that I'm not interested in being physical just yet, so why are you continually pushing when I've already said no?"

Walk Away

If someone continues to disrespect a client's boundaries, they are allowed to disengage. Protecting themselves is not rude. It's responsible.

Clinician Reflection

Before teaching clients how to say no, it can be useful to pause and reflect on your own relationship with this skill. As clinicians, many of us are helpers by nature, and that identity can quietly reinforce the same people-pleasing patterns our clients struggle with. (Sorry to call us out!) Noticing where saying no feels uncomfortable for you can honestly deepen your empathy and help you model this skill more authentically for your clients.

Let's also not forget to consider that a client's difficulty saying no may be less about a lack of skill and more about fear, attachment wounds, or learned survival strategies. For many clients, saying yes has historically meant safety, connection, or approval. Asking them to say no doesn't just feel assertive—it can feel risky. Even when the request itself seems minor, the perceived cost can feel big. It's always good to approach this work with compassion and empathy for the other person's lived experience.

Finally, remember that practice matters way more than performance here. Encourage clients to rehearse saying no in low-stakes situations to build their confidence and self-trust over time. Each successful no strengthens their ability to protect themselves without abandoning their relationships. Your role isn't to push them to say no perfectly, but to help them believe that honoring their needs is allowed—and doable—in baby steps!

Saying No with Confidence

Because saying no doesn't make you selfish

Being able to say no is one of the most important parts of maintaining healthy boundaries and balanced relationships. It may seem like a small skill, but without it, relationships can slowly start to feel overwhelming, one-sided, or draining. Imagine driving a car that only has a gas pedal and no brakes. You might keep moving forward, but you don't actually have much control over where you end up. Saying no gives you those brakes.

The good news (especially for those who identify as people-pleasers) is that there isn't just one way to say no! Some approaches work better in certain situations than others, and *you* get to decide which ones feel most natural and appropriate for you. The options on this worksheet offer different ways to hold a boundary depending on the moment.

Show Confidence

Notice this says *show* confidence, not necessarily *feel* confident. Fake it till you make it, babe! Most people don't feel confident the first few times they say no, especially when they are out of practice. What matters more is how the message is delivered. Sit or stand upright, make eye contact, and speak in a steady tone to help your boundary come across clearly. When people perceive confidence, they're less likely to keep pushing.

Next time you need to say no, what might help you show confidence?

____

____

Repeat Yourself Calmly (Broken Record)

Sometimes people keep pushing after you've already said no. How fun. In those situations, you can calmly repeat your answer without adding new explanations or getting pulled into a debate. Think of it like calmly pressing replay on the same sentence. This is an excellent option for people with whom you need to hold a boundary but to whom you don't owe an explanation. For example:

> FRIEND: "Come out tonight! You can just stop by for a little bit."
>
> YOU: "Thanks for inviting me, but I'm not able to make it tonight."
>
> FRIEND: "Come on, you've been working so much lately."
>
> YOU: "I know, but I'm still not able to come tonight."
>
> FRIEND: "Just one drink?"
>
> YOU: "I wish I could, but my answer is still no. Thanks for thinking of me."

How could you repeat your boundary calmly if someone keeps pushing?

____

____

Keep It Simple

Sometimes the most effective no is also the simplest one. You don't have to provide a long explanation or justify yourself. For example:

- "I appreciate you asking, but I can't."
- "That's not something I'm able to do right now."
- "I'm not comfortable with that."
- "That won't work for me."

The wording doesn't need to be perfect. Often, the hardest part is simply giving yourself permission to say it.

How might you say no clearly but simply in your situation?

____

____

Use Light Humor (When Appropriate)

In more casual situations, humor can sometimes help soften the moment while still holding the boundary. This works best in low-stakes situations where safety and power dynamics aren't a concern. For example:

- "Sorry, my couch and I have a date tonight."
- "I'd love to, but my energy level says absolutely not."
- "Oh, I wish I could . . . but I really don't want to."

How could you use a little humor while still holding your boundary?

____

____

Offer a Small Excuse (A White Lie)

If saying no directly feels uncomfortable right now, it's okay to give a simple reason that helps you hold the boundary. You don't need to share more information than you want to! Some stuff can remain private while you still hold the boundary. For example:

- "I already have plans."
- "I've got an early morning tomorrow."
- "I'm not feeling up to it tonight."

What simple responses could you use to protect your boundary without oversharing?

Give an Honest Reason

As this skill gets easier, you may feel more comfortable offering a straightforward reason for saying no. The key here is to be honest without overexplaining. One sentence is usually more than enough. For example:

> COWORKER: "Can you cover my shift tonight?"
>
> YOU: "Thanks for asking, but I need to focus on my own responsibilities right now."
>
> FRIEND: "What are you drinking tonight?"
>
> YOU: "I'm actually not drinking these days."

What is an honest reason you could share when saying no?

Offer an Alternative Option

Sometimes no doesn't mean you don't want to help at all. It just means the original request doesn't work for you as is. Offering an alternative can keep the connection while still respecting your limits. This is your "I can't swing that, but I can swing this" option. For example:

- "I can't attend the event, but I'd be happy to help you plan it."
- "I'm not able to lend money, but I'd gladly help you look over a budget."

What alternatives could you offer in your situation?

Buy Yourself Some Time (Assertive Delay)

Spoiler alert: You're allowed to pause before giving an answer. Not all requests need an immediate answer. Taking time to think about the request is a boundary in itself. You don't have to decide anything immediately! For example:

- "Let me check my schedule and get back to you."
- "I want to think about that before I answer."
- "I'll let you know tomorrow."

How could you give yourself time before responding?

Address the Pattern of Confrontation

If someone repeatedly ignores your boundaries, it may be helpful (and time) to name what's happening directly. Bringing attention to the pattern can help reset the conversation. Some people don't notice when they are pushing your boundaries, while some do and need to be called on it. For example:

- "I've already said that I'm not interested, and it feels uncomfortable that you keep asking."
- "Why are you continually pressuring me when I've already said no?"

If someone keeps pushing after you've said no, how could you address it directly?

Remove Yourself

If someone continues to ignore or disrespect your boundaries, you're allowed to simply disengage. Protecting your well-being is not rude. Sometimes the healthiest choice is simply to step away from the interaction.

How will you know when it's time to walk away?

Final Reflection

Think of a recent time when you wanted to say no but didn't, or when you said yes even though you didn't want to. What made it difficult to say no in that moment?

Which of the approaches from this worksheet feels most doable for you right now?

What might it sound like to say no in a way that respects both you and the relationship?

Remember: Saying no is a skill, and like any skill, it gets easier with practice! It's not something that either you have or you don't. It's built with time and practice. Each time you honor your limits, you build trust with yourself. My advice here is to try practicing in small, low-pressure situations first. Maybe tell a friend you're staying in tonight instead of pushing yourself to go out when you're exhausted. You might be surprised to find that the world doesn't fall apart when you say no. The relationship survives. And you begin to learn that your needs matter too!

How to Receive Feedback in a Healthy Way

How to hear feedback without spiraling, shutting down, or going on the defensive

In interpersonal effectiveness, as much as the goal is to become an assertive badass, it's also about being able to receive other people's boundaries and their nos with grace. I find that this part gets lost on some, so here I am giving it the spotlight it deserves. Receiving feedback is one of those things that sounds simple in theory but feels brutal in practice. Most clients don't struggle with feedback because they are immature, fragile, or unwilling to grow. They struggle because feedback often activates a threat response in the nervous system. Threat for what, you might ask? Anything! Threat of abandonment, dislike, rejection, authority trauma, emotional invalidation, criticism. The list goes on.

Because of this full-body nervous system response, clients who receive feedback can go into fight, flight, or freeze mode. Fight shows up as defensiveness, arguing, interrupting, or counterattacking. Flight shows up as shutting down, dissociating, people-pleasing, or mentally checking out. Freeze shows up as blankness, silence, or feeling suddenly stupid.

I often tell clients that the goal of this skill is not to love feedback (because who does?), agree with all feedback, or immediately change based on feedback. The goal is to stay regulated enough to take in the information, decide what is useful, and protect self-respect in the process. Receiving feedback well is mostly about regulation, then discernment.

A helpful reframe for clients is this: "Feedback is data, not a verdict. Some data is accurate and useful. Some data is incomplete, biased, or just plain nonsense. Learning to receive feedback skillfully allows you to sort through that data without collapsing into shame or launching into defense."

When you introduce this skill, it can help to normalize how hard it is. I'll often say something like "If feedback instantly makes your chest tighten or your stomach drop, that's a normal human response! That's your nervous system reacting to perceived threat." That validation alone can lower resistance and open the door to skill use. And to be honest, feedback is never fun to hear, no matter how skilled you are at hearing it.

The accompanying client-facing worksheet breaks this skill into concrete, doable steps, which is key for those who need real practice with this. Clients who struggle with feedback often need structure in the moment because their Wise Mind goes offline fast. Walking through these steps ahead of time allows them to rehearse a different response before they're emotionally flooded. Here are the steps and how to explain them with clients.

Step 1: Brace Yourself

The first piece, bracing yourself, is especially useful for clients who tend to be blindsided by feedback. When they can anticipate feedback, it gives them a sense of control and reduces emotional vulnerability. This is also a great place to integrate their PLEASE skills. Feedback hits harder when they are hungry, exhausted, stressed, or already dysregulated. Helping clients see that can be empowering for them.

Step 2: Assume Positive Intent

Assuming positive intent is another key piece, and one that often needs nuance. For clients with relational trauma, this step can feel unrealistic or even unsafe. I like to frame it as a "working hypothesis" rather than a belief. We are not saying everyone has good intentions. We are saying, "Let's assume neutral-to-positive intent long enough to hear the information." Innocent until proven guilty type vibes. And if the feedback turns out to be unhelpful or malicious, then clients still retain the right to discard it later.

Step 3: Practice Active Listening and Stay Calm

Staying calm and listening actively requires clients to go back to their mindfulness roots. This is an opportunity to coach clients on slowing the interaction down. Pausing, breathing, and listening without interrupting can prevent clients from having those knee-jerk reactions they might later regret. It can be super helpful to role-play this in session, especially for clients who tend to react quickly or emotionally. And don't skip the basics: Literally practice slowing down the breath, focusing on one thing, and grounding the body—anything that helps the nervous system settle. This takes things down just a notch so clients can hear what the other person is saying without reacting impulsively.

Step 4: Avoid Personalization

This one is the hardest part for clients who equate feedback with worth. This is where separating behavior from identity becomes critical. Reinforce that the other person's feedback is about the client's actions, patterns, or impact, not about who they are as a person. I often try to help clients reframe feedback from "Something is wrong with me" to "Something I did had an impact." That teeny shift can be incredibly regulating because behavior can be adjusted without attacking their self-worth.

Step 5: Express Gratitude and Reflect Afterward

Even though this might sound counterintuitive, expressing gratitude when someone gives us feedback can actually be quite empowering. We're not saying, "Thank you for telling me I am the worst." We're simply recognizing that giving feedback isn't easy either—and appreciating that they're trying to be direct and honest with us, as opposed to building quiet resentment. Clients can thank someone for feedback without agreeing with it too—because remember, two things can be true at once. That distinction is key, especially for clients who fear that politeness equals surrender. In reality, it's about self-respect and openness.

Step 6: Keep the Good, Trash the Bad

This step gives clients explicit permission to discard feedback that is unhelpful, unsafe, or ill-intentioned. This is especially important for clients who have internalized criticism or who grew up in environments where feedback was abusive rather than constructive. At the same time, when feedback feels fair, specific, and aligned with the kind of person they want to be, this step invites clients to keep what's useful and work toward small, realistic improvements. Framed this way, healthy feedback becomes less about self-attack and more about building skill, confidence, and mastery over time. Sometimes, when feedback is given in a productive way, it can even serve as a road map for improving the relationship. Teaching clients that *they* have the power to choose what they take in can be a deeply corrective emotional experience.

Step 7: Make a Plan

When clients decide that a piece of feedback is fair and worth working on, the next step is making a small, concrete plan. This doesn't mean overhauling their entire personality or fixing everything at once (which, let's be real, some people may feel compelled to do). It simply means identifying one or two specific behaviors they can practice differently moving forward. What would it look like to apply this feedback in daily life, in a realistic and manageable way? Framing feedback as a skill to practice, rather than a flaw to fix, helps clients stay out of shame and focused on growth. In doing so, feedback becomes something clients can actively use instead of something that sits unprocessed and quietly fuels self-criticism.

A final coaching note: Encourage clients to practice this skill with low-stakes feedback first. Not every piece of feedback needs to be a big emotional test. If clients are open to it, you can even encourage them to ask a safe person in their life to offer a small piece of feedback in a low-emotion situation, purely as practice. Think of it like stretching before lifting heavy weights! They are building skills here, and like any skill, this one gets stronger with time, repetition, and intentional practice.

How to Receive Feedback in a Healthy Way

How to hear feedback without spiraling, shutting down, or going on the defensive

Receiving feedback can feel uncomfortable, activating, and sometimes even threatening, especially if you've had past experiences where feedback felt unsafe. This worksheet is designed to help you slow the moment down, stay regulated, and decide what to do with feedback in a way that protects your self-respect and the relationship. Remember: Feedback is information, not a verdict.

Step 1: Prepare Ahead (If You Know Feedback Is Coming)

Sometimes you know feedback is coming. A work review is scheduled. A partner or friend says, "Hey, we need to talk." When that happens, preparation can make a big difference. Before the conversation, take a moment to check in with yourself.

What kind of feedback might come up?

____

____

What reactions do you notice as you think about it? (Examples: anxiety, defensiveness, dread, shutdown)

____

____

How can you support your nervous system beforehand? (Examples: eating, resting, grounding, reminding yourself you can handle this)

____

____

What intention do you want to bring into this conversation? (Examples: staying open, listening without interrupting, protecting your self-respect)

____

____

Step 2: Assume Neutral or Positive Intent (For Now)

You don't have to decide whether the feedback is accurate, fair, or helpful right away. That decision can come later. For now, the goal is simply to stay open long enough to hear the information without your nervous system going into full defense mode. Assuming neutral or positive intent is not about blindly trusting the other person or excusing harmful behavior. It's a temporary mindset that helps you stay regulated and gather information.

For the moment, ask yourself, "What might this person be trying to communicate, clarify, or improve?"

____

____

Step 3: Listen Without Reacting

In this moment, your job is not to agree, disagree, explain yourself, or correct the other person. Your job is simply to hear their message. This might mean slowing your breathing, unclenching your jaw, keeping your body still, or reminding yourself "I can respond later." Try to focus on the words being said, not the story your mind is creating about what they mean. Write down the feedback as neutrally as possible, without adding interpretation or judgment.

What was actually said? Imagine you are writing this down for a third party.

____

____

Step 4: Separate Behavior from Identity

Feedback is about how your actions impact others, not who you are as a person. Instead of telling yourself "Something is wrong with me," try finishing this sentence: "One thing I did that had an impact was . . ."

How can you reframe what was said to focus on the impact of the behavior, not your self-worth?

____

____

How does this reframe change how the feedback feels in your body?

____

____

Step 5: Express Appreciation (If It Feels Safe to Do So)

You can thank someone for being honest without agreeing with everything they said.

What could you say that feels authentic and respectful? (Example: "Thanks for telling me. I'll think about this.")

____

____

Step 6: Keep the Good, Trash the Bad

Not all feedback deserves to live rent free in your head. Some feedback is good and worthwhile; some is absolute garbage.

What parts of this feedback feel fair, specific, or useful?

What parts feel unhelpful, unsafe, or simply not true for you? Remember, you are allowed to discard what doesn't serve you.

Step 7: Make a Small Plan (If You're Keeping Any of It)

If some of the feedback feels valid, you don't need to overhaul yourself. One small step is enough. This helps give the feedback—and the emotions that come along with it—somewhere to land, as opposed to sitting in the self-shame abyss.

What is one specific behavior you could practice differently based on this feedback?

When or where could you try this out in real life?

How will you remind yourself that this is skill building, not self-punishment?

Final Reflection

What feels different after slowing this down and working through it?

What did you learn about how you respond to feedback?

Blocks to Interpersonal Effectiveness

How to identify the patterns that undermine relationships

Interpersonal effectiveness is often taught as a set of skills. DEAR MAN, GIVE, FAST. Ask clearly. Set boundaries. Respect yourself. Yada yada. But what gets less attention is this hard truth: Even when clients know the skills, there are habits and reflexes that can quietly (but quickly) sabotage them in real time. This section focuses on those blocks.

Disclaimer: Blocks to interpersonal effectiveness are not character flaws. They are learned strategies developed for survival, protection, or emotional self-defense. At some point in a client's life, these behaviors likely worked for them. They helped avoid conflict, reduce vulnerability, regain control, or protect against shame or rejection. The problem is that what once protected them now damages connection—connection that they have been working hard to establish through the previous interpersonal effectiveness skills. We don't want those to go to waste!

I like to frame these blocks as "automatic responses that hijack skillful communication." When emotions rise, our nervous systems activate, and old patterns take over before our new skills have a chance to intervene. That's why clients will often say, "I don't know why I said that" or "It just came out." That's likely a stress response for them.

Here it's important to balance accountability with compassion. As a clinician, you need to come at this with a nonjudgmental, validating stance, while also naming the elephant in the room: that these patterns may be hurting their relationships. The goal is to help clients recognize these behaviors, understand their impact, and take responsibility for changing them, without spiraling into shame or self-criticism. This kind of gentle, direct and behavioral awareness opens the door to actual change.

Another key point to emphasize is that these blocks to interpersonal effectiveness don't just harm the relationship. They also prevent clients from getting their needs met. Discounting, withdrawing, blaming, or derailing conversations might bring short-term relief, but they almost always backfire long term. So it's not just the relationship that pays the price. By continuing to engage in these patterns, clients end up hurting themselves too.

The accompanying client-facing worksheet walks through several common interpersonal blocks, including:

- Discounting
- Withdrawing
- Stonewalling
- Threatening
- Blaming
- Belittling
- Gaslighting
- Derailing

I often encourage clients to look for patterns across relationships rather than focusing on one incident. Do they tend to withdraw when conflict arises? Do they minimize others' emotions when they feel overwhelmed? Do they derail conversations when shame shows up? These patterns usually repeat because they are familiar, not because they are truly effective.

It's also important to distinguish between intent and impact. Many clients will say, "I didn't mean it that way." And honestly, that may be completely true for them! At the same time, the impact still counts. Growth and repair require holding two truths at once: They may not have intended to cause harm, *and* harm may still have occurred. (Look, another dialectic!)

While reviewing these patterns, it can be helpful to slow clients down and invite curiosity rather than defensiveness. The goal isn't to label them as "toxic" or "bad communicators," but to help them recognize patterns and their consequences. Sometimes a little self-disclosure can help normalize their experience. It's a gentle reminder that everybody who is a human has probably engaged in these patterns at some point or another. I know I have!

As you work through this material, remind clients that change doesn't require perfection. Even small interruptions or course corrections in these patterns can make a huge difference. Ultimately, it's about helping clients move from automatic, reactive responses to intentional, values-aligned interactions. When clients understand their blocks, they gain knowledge, and that knowledge can lead to choice. And that choice is where the magic of interpersonal effectiveness begins for many.

Blocks to Interpersonal Effectiveness

How to identify the patterns that undermine relationships

We all want to communicate better in our relationships. And even when we know the "right" skills to use, old habits have a sneaky way of creeping in and taking over. This worksheet is designed to help you spot those patterns with curiosity, not judgment.

As you move through this worksheet, remember: These blocks are not personality flaws. They're learned responses that tend to show up when emotions run high, conflict feels threatening, or vulnerability feels risky. This isn't a space for blame or self-shame—it's a place to notice patterns that might be disrupting all the hard work you've done to build healthy relationships. Understanding these patterns can make the most of your other skills!

Step 1: Notice the Patterns

The following is a list of common blocks to interpersonal effectiveness. Read through them and put a check mark by any that feel familiar to you. You don't need to identify with all of them. Most people recognize a few. And again, no judgments! You're just looking at behavioral patterns as a way to be more effective in your relationships moving forward. All of us do some version of these!

- ☐ **Discounting:** Minimizing, dismissing, or invalidating another person's thoughts or feelings, often unintentionally, in an attempt to quickly shut down discomfort. For example, someone shares how they feel and your response is something like "It's not that bad" or "You're overreacting."
- ☐ **Withdrawing:** Emotionally pulling away, shutting down, or creating distance instead of engaging in a conversation that feels uncomfortable or overwhelming. This often looks like emotionally checking out. For example, you stop sharing, give shorter responses, avoid eye contact, or suddenly become "too busy" to talk when something uncomfortable comes up. The other person feels the distance but doesn't always know why.
- ☐ **Stonewalling:** A more intense form of withdrawing where someone shuts down completely and refuses to engage or respond at all. This can look like giving no response, not engaging, or even walking away mid-conversation.
- ☐ **Threatening:** Using fear, ultimatums, or implied consequences to control an outcome instead of communicating needs directly. For example, "If you don't change, I'm leaving" or "If you keep this up, you'll regret it." The goal is control or compliance rather than understanding or problem-solving.
- ☐ **Blaming:** Shifting responsibility entirely onto the other person, often ignoring complexity or your own role in the situation. For example, "This is all your fault" or "If you weren't like this, we wouldn't have issues." It usually leads to defensiveness rather than resolution.

- ☐ **Belittling:** Using sarcasm, condescension, or comments that make the other person feel small, incompetent, or inferior. For example, "You're so sensitive," "That's a stupid idea," or "You never get anything right." Even if said jokingly, it chips away at trust.
- ☐ **Gaslighting:** Manipulating someone into doubting their own perception, memory, or reality, often to avoid accountability or gain control. For example, "That never happened," "You're imagining things," or "You're crazy for thinking that." Over time, it makes the other person question their own reality.
- ☐ **Derailing:** Shifting the conversation away from the original issue, usually when shame or defensiveness arises, so the core problem never gets addressed. For example, someone brings up a concern, and your response is "Well, what about the time you . . ." or "You're not perfect either." The original issue never actually gets addressed.

Step 2: Get Curious, Not Critical

What are one or two blocks you notice yourself using most often?

____

____

When do these tend to show up for you? (Examples: during conflict, when you feel criticized, when emotions feel overwhelming)

____

____

What do you think this behavior is protecting you from in the moment? (Examples: rejection, shame, feeling out of control, emotional overwhelm)

____

____

Step 3: Notice the Impact

In the moment, these behaviors may feel relieving or protective. But over time, they often have a cost. How does this pattern tend to impact your relationships?

____

____

How does it impact your ability to get your needs met?

____

____

Step 4: Intent vs. Impact

Most of us don't use these behaviors with the intention of hurting others. They are old habits that we likely picked up early on, only now they're no longer serving us.

What is usually your intent when this block shows up? (Examples: avoid conflict, protect yourself)

____

____

How does your behavior impact the other person or the relationship? (Examples: the other person feels shut out, there is more arguing)

____

____

Holding both of these truths matters. You may not have had harmful intent, but the impact still matters.

Step 5: Interrupting the Pattern

Noticing these blocks is a big first step. The next step is knowing what to do instead when that urge shows up. Even small shifts can change the tone of a conversation! Think of these as skill swaps, not rules.

If You Notice Yourself . . .	Try This Instead . . .
Discounting (e.g., "It's not that bad," "You're overreacting")	"I can see why that felt stressful for you." "That makes sense given what you were dealing with." "Okay, I hear that this really bothered you." "I don't totally get it yet, but I can see it was a lot for you."
Withdrawing (checking out, getting distant, avoiding the conversation)	"I'm feeling overwhelmed and need a few minutes, but I want to come back to this." "I'm not ready to talk yet, but I don't want to avoid it." "I'm starting to shut down and I don't want to. I just need a minute." "I'm not ignoring this; I just need some space so I don't make it worse."
Stonewalling (shutting down completely, silence, walking away)	"I'm really feeling flooded right now. Can we take a break and come back to this?" "I need help slowing this down." "My brain is offline. Can we pause and come back to this later?"
Threatening (giving ultimatums, making fear-based statements)	"I'm scared this won't change, and that's why I'm reacting so strongly." "I need reassurance or a plan here, not a fight." "I'm reacting out of fear right now, not because I want to threaten you." "I need to talk about what I'm scared will happen, not fight about it."

If You Notice Yourself . . .	Try This Instead . . .
Blaming (telling the other person it's all their fault)	"I'm frustrated and I think I'm reacting strongly because I feel unheard." "I want to focus on fixing this, not on figuring out who's to blame." "I'm really frustrated and I know I'm pointing fingers right now."
Belittling (using sarcasm, condescension, cutting remarks)	"I'm feeling insecure and it's coming out sideways." "I'm upset and I want to talk about it directly." "That came out harsher than I meant it to." "I'm feeling defensive and it's making me snippy."
Gaslighting (dismissing someone's reality or memory)	"That wasn't my intention, but I hear how it landed for you." "We remember this differently, and your experience still matters." "I don't agree with everything, but I'm not trying to invalidate you."
Derailing (changing the subject, bringing up old issues)	"I'm having the urge to change the subject because this feels uncomfortable." "I'm tempted to bring up other stuff right now, but let's stick to this." "I know I'm deflecting. Let's stay on the original issue."

What is one early sign that this block is starting to show up for you? (Examples: tight chest, urge to shut down, racing thought, wanting to "win")

____

____

What is one skill swap you could try instead next time, even imperfectly?

____

____

Miscellaneous DBT Skills

Relapse Prevention Plan

How to plan ahead without assuming failure

Relapse prevention is one of those skills that can unintentionally bring up a lot of resistance for clients. Some hear the word *relapse* and immediately think, "You don't believe in me" or "You're assuming I'm going to mess up." I always like to reframe this assumption by telling clients that it's not that I don't trust *them*—it's that I don't trust the addiction, eating disorder, self-harm impulses, and so on, because we know how strong those can be. Sometimes, this helps shift them out of self-blame and allows them to see just how powerful some of these urges are. Relapse isn't a moral failure—for many, it's part of the process!

In DBT, relapse prevention is about being cautiously optimistic and planning for any concerns should they come up. I like to joke around and tell people that I look at it like a prenuptial agreement. When you're getting married, you hope you don't have to use it—but if you get divorced, you're going to want it! A helpful way to frame this for clients is to say, "We plan for hard moments not because we expect you to fail, but because we know you're human." Planning ahead reduces shame, increases agency, and gives clients options when emotions run high and access to skills might drop.

This skill is designed for anyone who is trying to move away from a behavior that no longer serves them, whether it's substance use, self-harm, disordered eating, impulsivity, or any other pattern they're actively working to curb. It's especially helpful for people in early recovery, during periods of transition, or when they're approaching known high-risk situations like holidays, social events, family gatherings, work stress, or big emotional milestones.

The accompanying client-facing worksheet walks clients through a "before, during, and after" framework. That structure matters because many clients only think about coping once they are in the heat of the moment—and by then, they are already overwhelmed. This skill helps them widen the window of intervention so that support and skills are available earlier, when they are actually more effective!

- **Before the event,** the focus is on preparation and protection. This includes identifying support people, setting accountability, planning exits, managing physical vulnerabilities with HALT or PLEASE skills, and being intentional about where they go, how long they stay, and what situations they expose themselves to. Clinically, this is a great place to reinforce that boundaries are preventive care, not avoidance.
- **During the event,** the emphasis shifts to accessibility. What skills can they realistically use in the moment? Who can they reach out to? What can help them stay grounded, distracted, or connected to their values? Having scripts, excuses, and escape plans ready ahead of time is key. When stress is high, decision-making capacity tends to drop. Pre-deciding removes pressure in the moment.

- **After the event,** the goal is recovery, reflection, and reinforcement. How's that for alliteration? This is where so many clients skip steps because they either white-knuckle through the situation and move on without processing it, or they beat themselves up afterward, without any real reflection and understanding of what happened. The post-event section helps clients intentionally debrief, notice what worked, learn from what didn't, and reward themselves for effort, not perfection. This reinforces progress and builds motivation rather than shame.

Pro tip: Relapse prevention plans are living documents. They can and should change over time as clients gain insight, confidence, and stability. A plan that works in early recovery may look very different six months later. Perhaps the client learned new skills that they like better than the old ones. Encourage clients to revisit and revise their plan regularly.

Client Worksheet

Relapse Prevention Plan

How to plan ahead without assuming failure

Relapse prevention is all about planning for hard moments so you're not left scrambling when emotions run high in tough situations. It's about preparing for reality. You're human, urges happen, and having a plan will most certainly give you options.

You can use this worksheet for anything you're working to curb, including substance use, self-harm, disordered eating, impulsive behaviors, or other habits that no longer serve you. It's also especially useful when you have an upcoming event that could trigger old coping mechanisms, such as holidays, family vacations, tough conversations, work events, social gatherings, anniversaries, or emotionally loaded milestones. Think of this plan as a living document. You're allowed to change it, update it, and ask for help building it out. Planning ahead is a skill where practice makes progress! Think of this as preparation, support, and learning as you go.

To start, identify what it is that you're preparing for. Is there a specific event, situation, time period, or trigger coming up that feels risky or difficult?

____

____

What behaviors or urges are you trying to avoid or reduce in this situation?

____

____

Before: Preparing and Protecting

Use this section to create a plan and increase your chances of success. Planning ahead gives you a stronger starting point.

Who can you reach out to if you need extra support?

____

____

Have you let them know this situation might be hard for you?

☐ Yes ☐ Not yet ☐ I plan to

Who or what can help keep you accountable?

____

____

What limits or boundaries can help protect you in this situation? Think about people, places, things, or situations you may want to avoid, as well as time limits you might want to set in advance.

How can you prepare your body and mind before entering this situation? (Examples: get enough rest, eat beforehand, stay hydrated, regulate your emotions, check in with yourself)

If the urge starts to get stronger, what is your exit plan? Where can you go, what can you do instead, or what step can you take to create some distance from the urge?

What can you look forward to afterward as a reward?

During: Getting Through the Moment

This section is about accessibility. What can you realistically do in the moment?

What skills or coping tools can you use right now? (Examples: ACCEPTS, positive coping thoughts, paced breathing, checking the facts)

Who can you contact if you need support?

What short statement or reminder can you use to interrupt the urge when it shows up? This could be something you say to yourself or to someone else. (Examples: "Not right now," "This urge will pass," "I'm choosing something different")

What scripts or skills for saying no can you use if you're feeling pressured or uncomfortable?

What is your mini escape plan if the urge starts to build but you're not ready (or able) to fully leave the situation? (Examples: stepping outside, changing rooms, distracting yourself for a few minutes, texting someone supportive, using a quick coping skill)

What is your full escape plan if the urge becomes too strong and you need to remove yourself from the situation entirely? Where will you go? What will you do instead? Who could you reach out to if needed?

What reminders can help you stay connected to why you're choosing recovery or change? (Examples: values, goals, loved ones)

After: Recovery, Reflection, and Reinforcement

This section is about taking care of yourself and learning from the experience. What you do after matters just as much as what you do during.

What went well? Effort counts, even if things weren't perfect!

What was hard or didn't work this time?

What can you adjust or add to your plan for next time?

How will you acknowledge or reward yourself for getting through this?

How will you physically and emotionally recover after this? (Examples: rest, food, movement, comfort, quiet time)

Dialectical Abstinence

How to stay committed to recovery without lighting it all on fire after a slip

Dialectical abstinence is one of DBT's most important recovery concepts, yet it's not talked about a lot. It's especially fabulous for clients who struggle with black-and-white thinking, intense shame after slips, or a pattern of "Once I mess up, I might as well fully relapse." At its core, this skill holds two truths at the same time: The goal is complete abstinence from the dangerous or maladaptive behavior, *and* if a slip does happen, the goal is to return to abstinence as quickly and safely as possible. This is dialectic heaven.

For one reason or another, many clients have been taught that recovery is all or nothing. You're either sober or you're not. You're either abstinent or you've blown it. While this mindset can feel motivating at first, it actually can become quite dangerous after a lapse because then shame floods in, hopelessness takes over, and clients think, "Okay, well, what's the point now?" That mindset is often what turns a lapse into a full relapse. Yikes!

Dialectical abstinence was designed to interrupt that exact cycle.

A helpful way to explain this to clients is to emphasize that dialectical abstinence is not "using in moderation" or "giving yourself permission to relapse." Some may initially interpret it as that, but you want to be crystal clear that it's actually a very firm stance of being 100 percent committed to abstinence—and also being 100 percent committed to getting back on track immediately if a slip happens. There is no window for giving up. There is no "Screw it, I've already messed up here."

I often say, "You are either abstinent, or you are actively working your way back to being abstinent." There is no third category. Period, the end.

This framing helps protect clients from the shame spiral that so often follows slips. Instead of asking, "Why am I like this?" or "What's wrong with me?" the focus shifts to "What do I do next?" That question keeps clients oriented toward action rather than self-attack. It really is the proverbial "Okay, what now?"

It's also important to explicitly contrast dialectical abstinence with rigid abstinence-only thinking. The goal in DBT is still full abstinence from the dangerous behavior. That part is not flexible. What *is* different is how clients should respond if a lapse happens. In more rigid models, a single slip can be treated like total failure. For clients who already struggle with shame or black-and-white thinking, that can unintentionally make things much worse. The moment they slip, the narrative becomes "Well, I've already ruined it," which can quickly snowball into a full relapse—because "Why not?" In the rooms of AA or NA, we call this the "screw-its" or the "F-its."

Dialectical abstinence takes a different approach. The standard still remains abstinence, but the response to a slip is practical and forward focused rather than catastrophic and dramatic. Instead of treating a lapse like everything is lost, clients treat it like a signal to immediately course-correct. Their mindset shifts from "I blew it" to "Okay, what's the next step to get back on track?" In other words, the commitment to abstinence is firm, but the response to imperfection is flexible. Clients don't lower the bar, but they also don't let one mistake light the whole recovery process on fire.

When teaching this skill, it's helpful to normalize slips without minimizing risk. You can validate that urges are powerful, habits are deeply ingrained, and recovery is rarely linear, while also simultaneously being clear that the behavior itself is dangerous or harmful. Both truths matter equally.

Another key teaching point is speed. Dialectical abstinence emphasizes getting back to abstinence quickly. That might mean a few things: reaching out for support immediately, reengaging coping skills, increasing structure, or revisiting a relapse prevention plan. The longer a client stays stuck in shame or secrecy, the harder it is to course-correct. You're trying to swoop in there and clear things up ASAP! Think of dialectical abstinence like a GPS recalculating. You took a wrong turn, but the system doesn't shame you or shut down. It just says, "Okay, let's reroute." The sooner clients listen, the easier it is to get back on track to where they are going.

Dialectical Abstinence

How to stay committed to recovery without lighting it all on fire after a slip

Dialectical abstinence teaches you to hold two truths at the same time: (1) your goal is full abstinence from this behavior and (2) if you slip, your goal is to get back to abstinence as quickly and safely as possible. There is no "screw it" category here! You are either abstinent or actively working your way back to abstinence. There is no third option. This worksheet is designed to help you put dialectical abstinence into action. It guides you to name a behavior you're working to change and create a concrete plan so that the slip doesn't turn into a full-blown relapse.

Step 1: Name the Behavior

What behavior are you working toward abstaining from? (Examples: substances, self-harm, disordered eating, behavior patterns that no longer serve you)

Why is abstinence from this behavior important to you?

Step 2: Understand the Dialectic

Instead of thinking in all-or-nothing terms, this skill encourages a more balanced mindset that helps prevent a single slip from turning into a full relapse. Here are a few examples of dialectical ways of thinking about recovery:

- My goal is complete abstinence from this behavior.
- Slips can happen because I'm human, not because I'm a failure.
- A slip does not mean I've ruined everything.
- If a slip happens, my job is to respond quickly, not perfectly.

Now try creating your own dialectical statements about recovery. Think about how you can hold both commitment and self-compassion at the same time.

What is one dialectical statement you want to remember?

Step 3: Your "Okay, What Now?" Plan

If a slip happens, speed matters. The goal is to course-correct quickly.

If a slip happens, what is the very first thing you will do?

____

____

Who are the people you will reach out to immediately?

____

____

What are the skills you will reengage right away? (Examples: opposite action, checking the facts, positive coping thoughts, radical acceptance)

____

____

What will you NOT do? (Examples: hide it, beat yourself up, disappear, give up)

____

____

Step 4: Getting Back on Track

Think of dialectical abstinence like a GPS recalculating. You took a wrong turn, but the system doesn't shame you or shut down. It just says, "Okay, let's reroute." The sooner you listen, the easier it is to get back on track to where you are going.

How will you help yourself return to abstinence as soon as possible? What would "listening to the GPS" look like for you?

____

____

What reminders help you stay focused on recovery instead of shame?

____

____

Conclusion

If you're reading this, I really just want to pause for a moment and say thank you.

Truly, and sincerely, thank you.

Thank you for choosing to spend your hard-earned money on this book. Thank you for taking the time to actually read it, reflect on it, and hopefully try some of these ideas out in your own work. I don't take that lightly, not for a second.

Being a clinician is not easy work. It's emotionally demanding and intellectually taxing, and it can make you feel wildly underappreciated. And yet, day after day, you still show up.

My hope with this book was never to turn anyone into a "perfect DBT therapist." It was to help break down some of the complex DBT concepts into something more palatable and human. Something you could actually bring into the room in a way that fits you and the clients you serve. If even one skill, reframe, or explanation from these pages made your work feel a little clearer or a little lighter, then this book did its job.

You are doing meaningful work, and you are making a difference, even on the days it doesn't feel like it. And the fact that you're here, still learning, still curious, still invested in doing right by your clients, tells me everything I need to know about the kind of clinician you are.

Thank you for letting me be a small part of your clinical journey. I'm really glad you're here.

Client worksheets are available as a PDF download at **www.pesipubs.com/doable**

Expanded Emotions List

Use this list to help identify your emotions with more precision. Sometimes naming the feeling is the first step toward understanding it.

Joy/Happiness

Alive	Delighted	Grateful	Optimistic	Satisfied
Amused	Ecstatic Encouraged	Happy	Overjoyed	Sparked
Buoyant	Energized	Hopeful	Playful	Thrilled
Carefree	Enthusiastic Excited	Inspired	Pleased	Uplifted
Cheerful	Fulfilled	Joyful	Proud	
Content	Glad	Lighthearted	Radiant	

Love/Connection

Accepted	Caring	Devoted	Respected	Trusting
Adoring	Cherishing	Fond	Safe	Understood
Affectionate	Close	Included	Secure	Valued
Appreciated	Comforted	Loving	Supported	Warm
Attached	Compassionate	Loyal	Supportive	Welcomed
Bonded	Connected	Protective	Tender	

Sadness/Grief

Anguished	Desolate	Drained	Hopeless	Pained
Blue	Despairing	Empty	Hurt	Shattered
Broken	Devastated	Gloomy	Lonely	Sorrowful
Crushed	Disappointed	Grieving	Low	Tearful
Defeated	Discouraged	Heartbroken	Melancholy	Withdrawn
Dejected	Down	Heavy	Miserable	

Anger/Frustration

Aggravated	Defensive	Hostile	Livid	Seething
Angry	Enraged	Impatient	Mad	Triggered
Annoyed	Fed up	Incensed	Offended	Worked up
Antagonized	Frustrated	Indignant	Outraged	Wrathful
Bitter	Furious	Irate	Provoked	
Bothered	Heated	Irritated	Resentful	

Fear/Anxiety

Afraid	Exposed	On edge	Startled	Uneasy
Alarmed	Frightened	Overwhelmed	Tense	Unsafe
Anxious	Horrified	Panicked	Terrified	Vulnerable
Apprehensive	Intimidated	Petrified	Threatened	Worried
Concerned	Jittery	Restless	Uncertain	
Dreadful	Nervous	Shaken	Uneasy	

Shame/Guilt

Apologetic	Disgraced	Humiliated	Self-blaming	Uneasy
Ashamed	Embarrassed	Inadequate	Self-conscious	Unworthy
Awkward	Exposed	Inferior	Self-critical	Worthless
Contrite	Flawed	Mortified	Sheepish	
Defective	Foolish	Regretful	Small	
Dirty	Guilty	Remorseful	Tainted	

Disgust/Aversion				
Appalled	Disgusted	Nauseated	Repelled	Skeptical
Averse	Displeased	Offended	Repugnant	Suspicious
Contemptuous	Disturbed	Put off	Repulsed	Turned off
Critical	Grossed out	Queasy	Revolted	Uncomfortable
Disapproving	Judgmental	Repelled	Sickened	
Loneliness				
Abandoned	Disconnected	Invisible	Overlooked	Unseen
Alienated	Distant	Isolated	Separate	Unsupported
Alone	Excluded	Left out	Separated	Unwanted
Cut off	Forgotten	Misunderstood	Unimportant	Withdrawn
Detached	Forsaken	Outcast	Unnoticed	
Confusion/Uncertainty				
Baffled	Disoriented	Lost	Puzzled	Uncertain
Bewildered	Distracted	Mentally stuck	Questioning	Unclear
Chaotic	Foggy	Mixed up	Scattered	Unsure
Conflicted	Hesitant	Overwhelmed	Stunned	
Confused	Indecisive	Perplexed	Torn	
Stress				
Burdened	Exhausted	On edge	Pressured	Stretched
Burned out	Frazzled	Overloaded	Restless	Swamped
Depleted	Fried	Overstimulated	Scattered	Tense
Drained	Maxed out	Overworked	Spent	Wiped out
Drowning	Mentally tired	Preoccupied	Strained	
Calm/Peace				
Anchored	Comforted	Reassured	Secure	Still
At ease	Composed	Regulated	Serene	Tranquil
Balanced	Content	Relaxed	Settled Soothed	Whole
Calm	Grounded	Restored	Stable	
Centered	Peaceful	Safe	Steady	
Hope/Empowerment				
Able	Confident	Encouraged	Powerful	Self-assured
Bold	Curious	Fearless	Proud	Strong
Brave	Determined	Grounded	Purposeful	Unstoppable
Capable	Driven	Motivated	Resilient	Willing
Competent	Empowered	Optimistic	Resourceful	
Numb/Shutdown				
Blank	Disconnected	Empty	Muted	
Checked out	Distant	Flat	Numb	
Detached	Emotionless	Frozen	Shutdown	

Acknowledgments

This book would not exist without the support, guidance, and belief of some really important people in my life.

First, I want to thank PESI for taking a chance on me and allowing me to be part of a team I am genuinely so grateful to be a part of. It means more than I can fully put into words.

I also want to acknowledge Marsha Linehan, whose tireless work laid the foundation for everything in this book. DBT has changed the way I practice, teach, and connect with clients, and I'm incredibly grateful to be able to build on that work in a way that feels authentic to me.

To my former supervisors, Nick and Laura Lessa, thank you for seeing something in me early on and giving me the opportunity to grow. You helped shape me into the clinician I am today, and I carry that with me in every session and in every page of this book.

To all the clients I've had the privilege of working with over the years, thank you for trusting me, showing up, and doing the hard work. You are the reason I've been able to learn, refine, and truly understand how to make these skills real and usable in everyday life. This book exists because of you.

To my family, my mom, dad, and sister, thank you for being such a fiercely loving and unconditionally supportive foundation in my life. Your unwavering belief in me has allowed me to believe in myself. I would not be who I am today without you.

And finally, to Mimi, my girl, my constant, my little life force. You bring so much joy, comfort, and perspective into my life every single day. You remind me to slow down, be present, and lead with love, and for that I will forever be grateful.

About the Author

Lexi Mulee, LMHC-D, C-DBT, is the founder and owner of Wise Mind Counseling, a DBT-based private practice in New York City. She specializes in DBT and applies it in her work with individuals navigating borderline personality disorder, eating disorders, and substance use disorders, with a particular passion for supporting LGBTQIA+ youth.

Lexi earned her undergraduate degree from Hofstra University and her graduate degree from the University of Miami. With more than a decade of experience across inpatient and outpatient settings, she believes that effective therapy is never one-size-fits-all. Her approach is highly individualized, strengths-based, and deeply collaborative, rooted in the DBT principle that client and clinician are equal partners, rowing together toward the client's goals.

Beyond her clinical work, Lexi enjoys speaking and teaching, and is known for her dynamic, relatable, and engaging teaching style. Whether through storytelling, humor, or interactive exercises, Lexi works to make even the most complex concepts feel accessible, inspiring, and fun to learn.